Dedication

This book is dedicated to the one true and living God. He is my personal Lord and savior. Without Him I would be nothing. With Him I can do all things.

Reviews

For me, this writer's humor and personal experiences have the power to inspire every woman to "Get Organized" both naturally and spiritually!
— Sarah W.

This book is such a treasure, from the moment it starts! Even the acknowledgments had me in stitches! Dr. Katherine Hayes truly brings God's word to life in this aesthetically pleasing piece of art! Not only embodying the lessons of Christ's teachings but she also inserts her own personal experiences as well! They can be both gut wrenchingly sad as well as hilariously funny. She doesn't hold back and her well thought-out questions urge you to do the same. This bravely and well-written book is a must-have in the life of a Christian woman struggling to find her femininity in Christ!
— Audrey S.

With wit and humility, this author shares real-life experiences and offers practical insights from the word of God to help us look our best from the inside out. This book showed me that just as I put effort into what I look like, and choose to wear, I should be equally concerned to be beautiful spiritually and prepared for the challenges of life. Great read, I highly recommend.
— Donna G.

This study helped me to look into myself in a way that I never have before. The stories the writer shares about her own life are so honest and transparent. I looked forward to each new chapter! The scriptures, she has applied are all so insightful and encourages you to know that you can trust God, as He is always in control. Dr Katherine's own walk with Christ as outlined is such an inspiration! Having been thru so much herself, she not only maintains a brilliant sense of humor, but also such a wealth of knowledge of God's awesome word. I'm so glad she wrote this book to share with the world!

— Yvonne H.

Reading this book takes me back to a time when I wanted to please everyone, dress for others, wanting the approval of all. How often I clung to the things of this world without worrying if I could help someone else, besides myself. Today I know I've cleaned my spiritual closet. This book makes me travel to the past to see just how much God has transformed me. In fact, this book makes me feel a lot braver about my past and sharing with others because the author is so honest about hers. I'm thankful for this author's life, for writing such a book without pages that are torn or missing, teaching us that even being imperfect we are perfect in the eyes of the Father when we put on Christ. Just as God clothed Adam and Eve, He wants to clothe us. He has the perfect black dress for each of us. Thank you for teaching us to be authentic knowing that the most important dress of is that of a true disciple of Jesus.

— Marcia M.

God's Little Black Dress for Women: How to Put on the Armor of God without Losing Your Femininity

Author: Dr. Katherine Hutchinson-Hayes, Ed. D.

Editor: Jacqueline Persandi

Published by Lulu, http://www.lulu.com, 860 Aviation Parkway Suite 300, Morrisville, NC 27560

First Printing: 2016   ISBN: 978-1-365-19690-4   Content ID: 18723332

Original Cover Concept: Yolissa Bobb, U.S.A.
Cover & Interior Design: Roxanne M. Lee, U.S.A., roxlee@runbox.com

http://www.godslbd4women.com

If you have a question regarding content of this book, or would like to obtain more copies of this book, please contact khutcho767@gmail.com

Printed in the United States of America.

HOW TO PUT ON THE FULL ARMOR OF
GOD WITHOUT LOSING YOUR FEMININITY

Dr. *Katherine*
Hutchinson-Hayes, Ed.D.

God's
Little
Black
Dress
for women

Acknowledgements

There are several people I would like to thank for their role in the writing of this book.

There have been many family members and friends who have been a supportive blessing to me throughout a difficult season of writing, however, there are those, I would like to specifically thank. Many family members and friends have been supportive blessings to me throughout a difficult season of writing, however, there are those, I would like to specifically thank.

My mother Pauline Hutchinson has always been my number one fan and the best mother I know on this earth. She is truly a Proverbs 31 woman and I am proud to call her "mom." Although my father is deceased, he was an integral part of this book as he instilled in me long time ago a love of father figures, poetry, literature and the Bible. I must give a huge shout out to my prankster husband Tony Hayes who keeps me laughing and is supportive and generous beyond reason. Of course, I don't know where I'd be without each of my daughters, Zaji, Kesia, Sanne, (Nique) for believing in their mama and allowing her to do her thing! I also give God thanks for having a sister like Sophia Hutchinson who is not afraid to give both love and honesty in her critiques.

I am eternally grateful to my pastor Chuck Peterman and his wife Dana of Creekside Christian Church for allowing me to pilot this project over the course of two years. Their support, kindness and wisdom I welcome in this life. Roxanne Lee, your talent in graphic design and dedication to the mission field never ceases to amaze me. Yolissa Bobb, thank you for the vision to create the first visual mock-up of everything I had in my head. You got the ball rolling! Jacqueline Persandi, blessings for your skills in editing and fast turnarounds.

I must give some love to my pet family who kept me company late at night and early in the morning. At times, my cat Brownie would actually sit on my keyboard and stroke my face with her paws. This wasn't exactly helpful, but it was entertaining and it did keep me up because I had to stay alert enough to erase everything her tail typed. Her son, Tux, hung out with my rhinestone-collared dog, Sasha. This is the same rescue dog that I make promise me at least once a week that she will meet me in heaven one day. This cat and dog duo kept my feet warm and my trips to the fridge accompanied. Last but not least, a million of my most sincere thanks to the incredible women of the Alive Bible Study Women's Group for their feedback, food, fun and fellowship. Just thinking about this group makes me smile until my face hurts.

Foreword

"A woman's dress should be a like a barbed-wire fence: serving its purpose without obstructing the view."
—Sophia Loren

To me going out in the armor of God sounds clunky and unattractive. Seriously, where do we find the femininity in adding 20 pounds to our existing frame? Many of us, if we're honest, believe that the armor Paul described in the Bible sounds excessively Roman soldier-like for our tastes. Yet, just because he described this masculine suit to protect a soldier literally and a Christian spiritually doesn't mean that God wasn't thinking of us as females when he desires to "dress" us for the battles of this life.

Many women are searching for the right "dress" that can define who we really are or should be. The armor of God doesn't have to be a tough suit keeping everyone at bay, it can be what every woman desires and that is to be beautifully put together, and to attract all the blessings God has in store for each of us.

Yes! We can wear the armor of God with flair, style and function. In this book, learn how God tailor-makes a "little black dress" for each of us to fit every occasion. The Bible demonstrates that he has an armor for us that is every bit as protective and strong as a Roman soldier's armor while being every bit as feminine and flexible as a fabulous black dress!

In our effort to fill the roles that our society and our own sin has forced on us, have we lost the vision God designed us for. Can we be spiritually and relationally strong while being feminine? In this book, discover how God's design for women has not changed and how we can wear the black dress with confidence and power influencing others toward great purpose.

Table of Contents

Introduction

"Fashions fade, style is eternal." —*Yves Saint Laurent*

Do you ever feel like you've run out of options in your spiritual closet? Do you find yourself, as a Christian believer, overdressed, underdressed or dressed up with no place to go? Do you even know what it is to be dressed spiritually and how to put on the armor of God? Are you like me where you just want to say "good riddance!" to all of your dated, raggedy clothing or knockoff designer duds to be clothed with some real-deal godly wear?

This book takes us all the way back to the first runway when Adam and Eve came strutting down the catwalk decked out with the clothing designed for them by God himself. We examine how this happened and why we would have all messed it up. We get to see that God has women on his mind all the time and he desires a relationship with us through dressing us to walk with him in style and all the while. This journey is one where we walk together through scripture and the pages of real-life struggles to be dressed beautifully and fearfully made!

...it really

was the perfect

black dress. It

accented all the

right curves,

hid the bulges

and showed off

my legs just

enough...

Chapter 1

The History of the Little Black Dress

*"One is never over-dressed or underdressed
with a Little Black Dress."*
—*Karl Lagerfeld*

If you're anything like me, you're interested in relationships. Personally, I'm always on the scout for a few good girlfriends to knit souls with, how about you? I wondered if we could spend some time together. I'm a talker. I haven't always been this way. I used to be shy, but now I don't mind taking the lead. I'm also a great listener. But, this time, I want to pour into you some things that have been on my heart lately. I have a few secrets to share down the line, as we get closer. And, I even have some questions for all of us. I've always been inquisitive. I guess I was just built that way. I want to get to know you. Do you think that would be all right?

I'd also like to know what's going on with us women lately. I've been really looking at many of us and I'm wondering why we're so unhappy and lost? In addition, when did it become okay to shed our God-given femininity? I'm talking about us Christian women. Be honest with me. When was the last time you felt focused in God's plans for your life and delighted with yourself? When did you last feel beautiful without a stitch of make-up?

Do you think we could pitter-patter hand in hand into that land of a girl's child-like mind where anything is possible? I'd like for you and I to play dress up for real. If you'd allow me the chance, I think I have just the godly attire needed for us to experience a magnificent makeover. From sorting through many of the burdens and problems women struggle with, I found accessories and material from the Word of God to help each of us unmask even the best lies. The apostle Paul appears to have contemplated this issue of deception within the congregation often. He wrote to church members who were probably a lot like us in the 11th chapter of second Corinthians. I'm sure this group included well meaning, Bible-study girls who took cakes to cookouts and sang in the choir, but whose hearts were rotting at the core. He compared their spiritual state to that of Eve's when she was deceived in the garden by "the cunning serpent." He warned them that, like Eve, their minds were being "led astray from sincere and pure devotion to Christ" in an easy enough manner whenever they received a different spirit or gospel. Later in the chapter, he warns them to be on guard as there are those who, like Satan, "masquerade as an angel of light" (2 Corinthians 11:14). I learned through years of spiritual dress issues like, "I think this Bible makes me look fat," and "sin sort of looks good on me," —I was deceived!

Let me explain. Ladies, someone has been telling us that we've been looking lovely but they've been lying to us! Whatever it is we're wearing that has us in bondage, depressed, unlovable and unfulfilled, out of control and self-centered we need to take off and throw in the trash. Girlfriends, we're all in need of spiritual style that will take our soul to the best-dressed level. Then, we can wear the finest freedom, contentment, love, joy, confidence and peace. I can't wait to see the transformational power of the Word of God when we take off the rags of lies and deception and put on the regality of genuineness and truth. Our hearts are going to be some kind of beautiful.

I recall feeling beautiful while the sunset over Long Island cast a pink glow over my parent's snow covered lawn. It was a long time ago when my firstborn was two and she loved me without condition. Nevertheless, 17 years changes everything. My mother was babysitting for me after working the night shift at Kings County Hospital in Brooklyn. When I ran in her legs were propped on the kitchen table and she was rubbing her swollen ankles. Already, her white uniform was stained yellow with curry powder and flecks of red scotch bonnet peppers. A cast iron pot on the stove gurgled sending the smell of cooking chicken into my path. My stomach rumbled and I stared longingly at the pot while kissing my mom on the forehead. She pushed back long wisps of stray hair from her bun and gave me a one armed hug as she sipped her cup of tea with the other arm. Leaning forward she motioned for her granddaughter to climb onto her lap. "Hey mom thanks for helping me out tonight. I brought you and dad some groceries," I said and avoided looking directly into her dark circled eyes while quickly unpacking the bags. "Thanks honey. Is he going with you?" she asked. I clamped my lips tight then I said, "No." I managed not to let her see my hot face when I hurried out of the room.

I had taught all day as a 6th grade teacher and I should've been excited about a staff party I had to attend that same evening. On a teacher's salary, a discounted steak dinner, live music and a country club atmosphere was almost as good as a snow day. I rushed upstairs to get dressed. I examined the outfit I purchased for the occasion from a custodian who sold impeccable knock-off designer clothing from the trunk of his car. Gazing at the exquisite fabric, I thought again of the custodian who opened for business in the employee parking lot on Fridays the year prior. It was a great situation for the financially challenged staff and the custodian. At the time, he needed money for a custody battle he eventually won against his ex. I silently thanked this man because it really was the perfect black dress. It accented all the right curves, hid the bulges and showed off my legs just enough to be sexy but classy.

I remember trying to stall as I climbed down the steps so slowly my father took a break from shouting at some other contractor on the other side of town. Using one of his crutches to push the door aside he stood with the phone pressed to his chest. He then gestured for me to kiss him on the cheek so I had to jog back up the steps. Muffled voices screamed against his pajama top. Ignoring them, he whispered to me in the crack, "I'm sorry I was busy when you came in but if you want, I'll make a batch of my tonic when I get off the phone. It'll give you plenty of Jamaican stamina." I thought about the wonderful concoction that I knew would make me feel great but I didn't need an arrest for driving under the influence and a colon cleanse on possibly one of the worst evenings of my life. I also remembered there would be no devoted husband to drive. "Ah dad, thanks, but I've got to get going. I'll take a rain-check this weekend." I said while my thoughts took over. I didn't want to end up like the librarian at the last party — passed out in the bathroom. The principal ended up taking her home. I tried to conjure up an excuse to tell my coworkers to explain my husband's absence but I couldn't think of one I hadn't used before.

When I was finally ready to leave, I reached down to give my baby a kiss and she said, "Mommy you look boo-tee-full."Her chubby arms reached for me and out of habit, I bent over and nuzzled the soft black curls spilling from her head with my chin. I looked into the brown smoke of her eyes with my face upside down from hers. I noticed how her gold skin shimmered against the backdrop of my dress. I was amazed she even knew such a big word and the smile on my face became heartfelt. My baby must've sensed this change within me because her lips curved into a soft pink crescent.

I straightened up and caught my reflection in the window as the sun made her graceful descent from the sky. My reflection showed a woman who knew canceling her fourth appointment with the divorce lawyer the next day was not an option. I saw a woman with drowning eyes who was beautiful in a black dress. It was the first time in months that I knew God had not forgotten me. His fingers of comfort reached through my reflection to stroke my face as an old friend would in times of trouble. My life was coming apart as I once knew it and I had no idea what I was doing. My husband had recently put a hole in the wall of our home before moving out most of his belongings. My marriage was crumbling by the millisecond; I had a pile of bills, a baby to raise and a life to get on living. But, somehow, stepping out into that snow covered evening with the word "boo-tee-full" draped over my shoulders, I knew me and that little black dress were going to make it.

Then and now, a little black dress is an essential style staple that almost every woman has in her closet. It's so commonplace it has a place in The Oxford Dictionary of English as of 2010 listed under the acronym LBD. What's unique about the little black dress is it's not trendy or ever out of fashion, it is a die-hard classic. Most of us would credit French designer Coco Chanel with the invention of the little black dress. She brought the concept of the dress out to the world of high fashion in an issue of Vogue dating back to only 1926. The specific black dress that made her iconic was simple, calf-length shown with a string of pearls. The magazine called it "Chanel's Ford." They were referring to Henry Ford's Model T car, which at the time was setting the standard for many American cars to come. The magazine also predicted that Coco Chanel's design would be "a sort of uniform for all women of taste."Throughout her life, Chanel remained outspoken and confident about the staying power of the LBD. She advised every smart woman to have one in her closet. "One is never over nor underdressed in a little black dress," she said. However, the Chanel quote most closely associated with the LBD is,"A girl should be two things: classy and fabulous."

In reality, designers of black dresses of all shapes and sizes were around and had always been there, even before Coco Chanel became famous for her creations. It would be unfair to say she invented this type of dress. However, she assigned the dress significance and purpose. She gave the dress the heart-beat of a woman so that it would forever be a timeless wardrobe essential. She also gave the little black dress a voice. The dress would remain a symbol of female empowerment. It was the midst of the feminist movement when the rise of the term the LBD came about.

The rise of the LBD was a time when women were redefining what it was to be a woman. Women were experiencing freedom and equality that were new to their time. It was no wonder women embraced the idea of the little black dress. Women got the right to vote just six years prior in 1920. The first U.S. Federally approved birth-control clinic opened in New York City in 1923. During this time, women were moving to big cities to seek out education and employment opportunities. Many of them were sharing apartments or living on their own. They were also working in diverse settings in an independent fashion that was historical. The women that Chanel appealed to were now self-sufficient in a way that somehow needed an identity and the little black dress helped to capture this new version of the modern day woman. It was during this time that the term "shopping" was considered a recreational activity. With the freedom of managing their own money and time, women could shop for things that were just for them. Chanel's inspirational designs are inspired "for such a time as this" (Esther).

Coco Chanel's inspirations stemmed from her past in Saumur France. Her real name was Gabrielle and she was the second illegitimate child of a laundrywoman and a peddler of clothes and underwear. Gabrielle's parents were married after she was born, and then had five more children. Their father sent Gabrielle's two brothers to be farm laborers, and Gabrielle and her two other sisters into an orphanage when their mother died at 31. At the time, Gabrielle was only 12. Soon, she began working as an apprentice to a tailor and it was here she learned the art of dressmaking. When she left the orphanage at 18, she worked as a tailor, and moonlighted as a singer at cafes and concert halls. The local soldiers who came to watch her gave her the nickname Coco.

Coco became successful by the world's standards but I wonder who she really was at the core. Did she embrace the tragic beginning of her past? When she designed the LBD was she in mourning for her mother and her lost childhood? Did she mourn her father who gave her up? Did she mourn the death of her lover Arthur Edward "Boy" Capel who helped finance the start of her business? Perhaps she mourned her name that was to be her life. It seemed fitting for her to shed the old Gabrielle, the one born out of wedlock into poverty and abandoned at an orphanage. I could also understand why she willingly adopted the new name "Coco" given to her by soldiers. I just wonder if she realized it was synonymous for the term "kept woman."If she did know what the name meant, I wonder if she accepted this as her identity, as her way of being a female, of being feminine.

How about you, have you ever mourned something so deeply that it affected you up until now? Has it affected the way you see yourself in a negative way? Does it influence your decision-making process in any way? Have you given yourself a chance to come before the great physician and receive the healing you need? I believe it might be that way for many of us. I know it was that way for me. When my marriage ended in divorce, I felt the emptiness of loss even though I was grateful to put that relationship behind me. Still, I had an urgency to fill my life with another relationship so I wouldn't have to feel the hurt quite so badly.

I thought I would be able to cut my former husband out of my heart like a skillful surgeon and it would go on beating the same. I never contended with other things. We had a child together and he would have to be a part of our lives. I also didn't give myself time enough to grieve and heal from a marriage that had caused much pain. God uses time to work on us but I filled the time with another relationship. Soon I was married again to someone that I chose for myself and God had never even met the man. Just imagine how that turned out? Can you think of a time in your life when you felt God wasn't working fast enough on your behalf so you helped him out? How did that work out for you?

In scripture, the Bible talks to us about this very thing. It took me years to realize that God was actually talking to me through the verses I'm sharing. The word tells us, "Therefore, as God's chosen people, holy and dearly loved, clothe yourselves with compassion, kindness, humility, gentleness and patience. Bear with each other and forgive one another if any of you has a grievance against someone. Forgive as the Lord forgave you. And over all these virtues put on love, which binds them all together in perfect unity (Colossians 3:12-17)."

Even now, as I reread these verses I'm still thinking, wow! God, no offense, but that's a lot of clothing going on there and all for people who don't deserve it. To put love on over all of all those virtues is an incredible act of faith! Even on the coldest of days I would overheat and meltdown if it wasn't for God who says "For I can do everything through Christ, who gives me strength (NLT Philippians 4:13)."

"Therefore, as God's chosen people. Holy and dearly loved, clothe yourselves with compassion, kindness, humility, gentleness and patience. Bear with each other and forgive one another if any of you has a grievance against someone. Forgive as the Lord forgave you. And over all these virtues put on love, which binds them all together in perfect unity."

Memory Verse – Philippians 4:13 NLT

"For I can do everything through Christ, who gives me strength."

Dr. Chapter 1 Teaching Highlights

1. The Bible demonstrates that God has an armor for women that is every bit as protective and strong as a Roman soldier's armor while being every bit as feminine and fabulous as a black dress.

2. Our minds are susceptible to distraction. This behavior prevents us from centering our worship and devotion to Christ. When this happens consistently, we go "astray" and lose our way from God. Many of us even go off and follow various spirits and gospels that are untrue.

3. Satan will often dress up and "masquerade as an angel of light" to trick us into thinking he is god-like and worthy of worship.

4. God wants us to wear the finest freedom, contentment, love, joy, confidence and peace.

5. God's "dress" for us can't be worn until we take off the rags of lies and deception and then put on the regality of genuineness and truth.

One of my earliest recollections of church was shortly after my family had moved from England to the United States. The quiet mid-morning service took place in the grass green living room of one of the church elders whose conservative members referred to as one of the "friends."I remember feeling comforted by the crocheted pieces that hugged a pair of couches on the frayed arms like beautiful bandages. The smell of strong tea and burned toast clung to the air and reminded me of our own family's one bedroom flat several city blocks away. However, the best part of our church was God was in our midst.

I really mean that God was, or who I thought to be God, was there. Every Sunday, without fail Mr. King would be the first one to arrive to church seated at the front of service. His presence seemed to command the room's attention. He always wore a crisp white shirt a black tie and a button down sweater. I could always see a reflection of myself in his shoes if I stood just right. When he spoke, I swore the tiny-yellowed chandelier above his head shook. His voice scared the children in church even more than my father's voice did.

Although "God" never smiled or laughed with any of us children, he always had paradise plums for us. This sweet and sour candy tasted and looked like exotic Caribbean fruit only the oval pieces were covered in powdered sugar. Even someone as shy as I was then found my way to the front of the room when Mr. King dispersed the paradise plums after service from a white paper bag.

When the small group of congregation members left the two-story Brooklyn brownstone to go home and enjoy the rest of their Sunday, I would always lag behind my parents to watch Mr. King walk down the long block into the glittering sun until he disappeared. Yet, I never saw what I was looking for. One day, my mother asked the question. "Why do you always watch Mr. King walk to the end of the block?" I answered, "Because I want to see how God gets back up into heaven."

This childhood memory is one my parents loved to share with their friends, especially the friends that actually knew Mr. King. It was clear from their reaction that they could see how a child would perceive this man to be God because he had a persona of holiness and he never seemed to show any outward emotion. He was impeccably dressed and had a booming baritone voice. Although he didn't speak to children much, he showed his kindness.

While recalling this story makes me laugh, something about it makes me sad. This childhood memory is a reminder that my relationship with God never matured even after I faced the reality that Mr. King wasn't God. For many years of my adulthood, I continued to see God as an austere distant man who was domineering and difficult to be close to even though he showed signs of kindness and generosity.

I now know that my once immature relationship with God affected my ability to integrate biblical patterns and principles into my own life. I saw the people in the Bible as almost transcendent; wrong thinking ruined my ability to relate to any of them but worst of all it alienated me from God himself.

This Mr. King, who I personified as God in childhood compares to the false light seen in religion when we fix our focus on religious figures and practices, which lacks the authenticity of relationship. The scripture 1st Corinthians 1:9 says: "God, who has called you into fellowship with his Son Jesus Christ or Lord, is faithful." The words here tell us to nurture a friendship with God as does 1 John 1:3, "We proclaim to you what we have seen and heard, so that you also may have fellowship with us. And our fellowship is with the Father and with his Son, Jesus Christ."

1. Describe the difference between practicing religion and practicing a relationship with God.

2. Do you see God relating to you on a personal level? Describe how you know Him and how He knows you.

3. Would you describe your relationship with God as close, distant or estranged?

4. List two or more areas you would like to mature in spiritually and tell how you will accomplish your goal.

Notes

_____

_____

_____

_____

_____

_____

_____

_____

_____

_____

_____

_____

_____

_____

_____

_____

_____

_____

_____

_____

_____

_____

We see the
following pattern
recurrently: God
sets us up for
success, the
enemy comes in
with deception,
we the people fall
for it...

Chapter 2

God, Designer of the Original Little Black Dress

*"Start at the top.
The bottom is always going to be there."*
-Edward Wilkerson

My mom has taken to finding friends on Facebook. She talked to me about a recent conversation she saw on her news-feed. "It's amazing to me to see how many people we know that don't believe in God." She said, maneuvering her wheelchair closer to the kitchen counter to fix me a cup of tea. "Who was cussing on Facebook this time mom?" I asked as I packed away my guitar and pushed hers into its place against the fireplace. "Someone was making fun of the Bible today. They said the story of Adam and Eve in the Garden of Eden is stupid. They said it's a setup to put two people in a garden then tell them not to eat fruit from one tree. The comments were just horri-ble. People said that God should've never even put the tree in the garden." Leaning against the counter I drank my tea and I thought about what my mom said as I prepared to leave. "So, what made you so upset?" I asked. She looked up at me and shook her teaspoon before stirring her tea. "They thought the Bible was a joke."

My mother gave me a lot to think about as I drove from our weekly guitar lesson to pick up my children from school. I thought about all the people in my life whom I knew weren't saved yet. I'd never uttered a word to them about God. I felt a slight pang of guilt. I couldn't help thinking the very reason my mother was upset was often why I didn't share the gospel message. I didn't want to seem like I was a joke.

Like many of you, I've spent a lot of time around educated people. With a bachelor's of English, masters of education, doctorate of supervision and leadership in education, I may even pass as educated myself. Although the more I learn is the more I realize I don't know. Still, most of us want to be valued as people who are both intellectual and rational.

Somehow, telling people that the reason we have it so hard nowadays is because God who busted Adam and Eve for eating from a forbidden tree kicked us out of the Garden of Eden doesn't sound very intellectual or rational. The story only continues to get worse in the logical department: It was because Eve, tricked by the devil, thought she could be more like God if she did. The devil, who was acting like a snake for some reason, just so happened to be hanging out in paradise with the sin-free couple. Eve then gave this fruit to her husband, Adam, who ate it and later blamed the whole thing on her. It helps to know that God originally made this man out of dirt and then God made Eve out of one of Adam's ribs.

I again felt awash with remorse as I thought of all the times I questioned my own faith because of how ridiculous this all sounded. I wondered how we as Christians ever continue reading the Bible with an opening story like this one. It is rife with the illogical. Yet, there is something so huge about it that you just know this simple, child-like story means so much more. As we continue to live and read the word, we begin to see that the scenario in the garden plays itself out repeatedly in the lives of historically accurate people, times and places as well as in our own. We see the following pattern recurrently: God sets us up for success, the enemy comes in with deception, we the people fall for it, we trade the authentic for a cheap replica, we suffer the consequences of our choices, with repentance we're forgiven and offered relief, if we don't repent we're not forgiven and suffer even more.

Another question people ask is why God would put the Tree of Good and Evil in a Garden anyway. And, if Adam and Eve were without sin could they act in a sinful manner? Lastly, why didn't Adam and Eve die after eating the fruit like God said they would? These are all questions I have asked myself. After all, prior to switching to becoming an English major I spent half of my time in undergraduate school as a science major among the highest percentage of atheists of any other department on campus. Logical questions plagued me continually and branched into my faith, especially in the area of creation versus evolution. As a hands-on person, I loved the sciences because it gives you data. It gives you stuff you could plunge your mind into and grasp on many levels. Yet, the more I learned, the more something nagged at me.

The chief challenge for the Big Bang theory is the Cause of the universe and the Origin of matter and energy within space—how space, matter and time unexpectedly came into being. In actuality, astrophysicists and other scientists don't have the slightest notion. They've never really been able to explain the origin of the original infinite mass and energy. They've never been able to explain why there is a universe in the first place. The fragility of how the universe is structured and an explanation of how if even one planet moved by a fraction it could throw everything into chaos, demonstrates that the Big Bang couldn't have been so random after all. The odds of this hypothesis are so high that it is illogical to believe it. All scientific evidence points to, is a highly sophisticated source creating the universe at some point, which is unknown to us. Throughout my life sensing God's presence and walking through the Word, I found insight on a much-debated topic that I'd like to share with you.

God gave us the gift of free will. He wants us to love him of our own accord. Love is action and through love, we demonstrate obedience. God is all-powerful. Still, he yearns for us to show our love for him by obeying his commands. For Adam and Eve their obedience and demonstration of love was simply to not eat from a certain tree. Although Adam and Eve were without sin, the Bible displays very clearly that it doesn't take much for the human heart to sway when not concentrating on the right things. "I the Lord search the heart and test the mind, to give every man according to his ways, according to the fruit of his deeds" (ESV Jeremiah 17:10).Satan tempts Eve by questioning God's intent in giving them a command. He phrases God's words in such a way as to mislead Eve into thinking that God is keeping her from something good and that she is some- how missing out. "You won't die!" the serpent replied to the woman. "God knows that your eyes will be opened as soon as you eat it, and you will be like God, knowing both good and evil" (NLT Genesis 3:4-5). However, the word tells us in the book of (ESV Romans 12:2) "Do not be conformed to this world, but be transformed by the renewal of your mind, that by testing you may discern what is the will of God, what is good and acceptable and perfect."

This is a reoccurring theme for those of us who fall to sin. We feel as if it's just not that fun to be a Christian and somehow God always wants to stop us from having a good time. When we allow the enemy to infiltrate our faith and God's will with questions or doctrines that conform the word of God it is wise to renew our mind to be able to discern what the will of God is. We do this by keeping company with fellow believers, reading the Bible, praying, and allowing the Holy Spirit to saturate our hearts and check our frame of mind. "The righteous should choose his friends carefully, for the way of the wicked leads them astray." (NLT Proverbs 12:26)

When I try to put myself in Eve's position, I often wonder why she thought she needed improvement since it seemed she had everything going for her. Yet, a part of me knows I can be like Eve, seeking the spectacular and overlooking the supernatural, in my life, with my family and in situations to miss how blessed I am. If most of us are candid with ourselves, I think we could see that we each have the capacity to be like this.

I'm always looking for a way to improve inwardly or outwardly. This quest for self-improvement is another reason we go to church, attend Bible studies and work on our spiritual armor — wouldn't you agree? Well, sometimes we need a renewed perspective on things especially when life tends to get us down and it begins to show even in the way we dress. There are times when my gym membership never gets used, I despise all my clothes, my closet becomes cluttered, and I feel disconnected from God and so in need of a makeover.

"...a recent study in the Journal of Experimental Psychology elegantly demonstrates the way clothing and costumes affect us. The study, conducted by two professors at Northwestern University's Kellogg School of Management in Chicago, had two sets of people wear the same white-coat. One group was told the coat belonged to a doctor and the other group was told the coat belonged to a painter. The group wearing the "lab coat" showed a sharp increase in their ability to pay attention, while the group in "painter's coats" showed no improvement whatsoever. The study revealed that in terms of how clothing affects our feelings, it's less about the actual clothes we wear and more about what we associate with them. Their symbolic value and emotional attachments give them meaning. The white-coat study speaks to why we hang onto our dad's moth-eaten sweater and why we wear a killer black dress to a high school reunion. These decisions are not superficial. When you wear something that makes you feel great, the effects may be subtle — the way you tilt your head, your facial expressions and your body language — but they matter. It sends a message that you care about yourself. When we look good, we feel good — and vice versa."
(Enclothed Cognition: How Clothes Can Make Us Feel Better,

Smarter, and Empowered, By Samantha Boardman, MD,
Everyday Health Contributor, 10/1/2012)

Before there ever was a Macy's or Dillard's, the serpent was the first salesperson that skillfully slid up to Eve in the perfect isles of the garden and made a pitch that had poor Eve's knees weak. Maybe he modeled clothing to extraordinary background music and compared it to the finery that God wore. Perhaps he spoke with a powerful persuasive voice and all the appearance of wisdom. Eve wanted what the serpent said she could have by just paying the special sale price of the day marked down just for her ticketed as "disobedience," but the fine print read "man will be cursed forever." Isn't this still the tactic of the enemy? When he can't make inroads anywhere else he does it by an imitation of God and entices with an excellent sale pitch so loud we don't bother to read the fine print of the consequences of our decisions. I often think of my custodian friend who sold imitations of designer dresses and would show pictures of gorgeous celebrities dressed in the originals. He would then snag sales from most of his customers when he compared the savings of hundreds if not thousands of dollars if we bought from him. No matter how good of a copy we purchased — we knew it was always second best.

I think of friends and family I've known over the years that left the church to follow a false gospel. They fell for an imposture of God. Some even now sit on church pews sing the hymns and smile the smiles but in their hearts, they left the church a long time ago. Are you that person? When was the last time you checked your spiritual pulse? One family I knew who were all once very close really fought against each other and struggled over the issue of gay marriage. It was a difficult time for each of them and it caused division among the parents and the children. Let me explain. The siblings of the family did condone the marriage of their sister to her girlfriend because they saw that this new relationship seemed to make their sister much happier than they'd seen her be in years. However, the parents of the sister and the sister's children were deeply hurt because the marriage caused her to divorce her estranged husband and abandon the reconciliation they were all hoping would happen.

"Because of this, God gave them over to shameful lusts. Even their women exchanged natural sexual relations for unnatural ones. In the same way, the men also abandoned natural relations with women and were inflamed with lust for one another. Men committed shameful acts with other men, and received in themselves the due penalty for their error" (Romans 1:26-27). This passage is a New Testament depiction of God's contempt for sinful practices namely, homosexuality in a vivid manner leaving no room for interpretation. This scripture references the parents used to condemn her choice in lifestyle.

It was clear the parents felt strongly, but their children had equally strong viewpoints and together they couldn't find common ground. Not knowing what else to do and refusing to be involved in their daughter's wedding the parents cut off all ties to their children when their children became openly combative. The Bible condemns sexual immorality. However, it does the same with equal passion to the following behaviors as exhibited by my friend's family, "Furthermore, just as they did not think it worthwhile to retain the knowledge of God, so God gave them over to a depraved mind, so that they do what ought not to be done. They have become filled with every kind of wickedness, evil, greed and depravity. They are full of envy, murder, strife, deceit and malice. They are gossips, slanderers, God-haters, insolent, arrogant and boastful; they invent ways of doing evil; they disobey their parents; they have no understanding, no fidelity, no love, no mercy. Although they know God's righteous decree that those who do such things deserve death, they not only continue to do these very things but also approve of those who practice them" (Romans 1: 28-32).

The relationship between my girlfriend and I was truly stretched during this time. She was grateful for a level of transparency between us that was authentic. Yet, she was confused about my love for her and willingness to be friends while still disagreeing with her lifestyle. She grew impatient with what she described as "a lack of tolerance" for her lifestyle since I was honest with her about my position and why. Yet, she was also appreciative of me not casting judgment but rather using simple support from the word. My friend was disappointed that her parents weren't supportive of her sexual preference but more than that was the complete rejection she felt from them. Even after the parents rekindled a relationship with their children and grandchildren, they'd severed ties with her. She often called me to wonder aloud, "If my parents are Christians, how can they speak into my life without a relationship with me?" I thought the same thing.Even better, the Bible tells us that God wants us to treat everyone without partiality and or prejudice. "My dear brothers and sisters, how can you claim to have faith in our glorious Lord Jesus Christ if you favor some people over others?" (NLT James 2:1). In addition, the words confirms, "Yes indeed, it is good when you obey the royal law as found in the Scriptures: Love your neighbor as yourself. However, if you favor some people over others, you are committing a sin. You are guilty of breaking the law. For the person who keeps all of the laws except one is as guilty as a person who has broken all of God's laws" (NLT James 2:8-10).

As a mother, I understand the pain of sorting through a child's choices. Not all of my children are adults yet and I continue to grow in Christ as I watch them make their own decisions. This may be from deciding to pour too much juice into a cup, to deciding to get one's nose pierced. I have the unique position of being momma to three biological children all of who are girls — ages 19, 14, 6. I also have a 20-year-old daughter I embrace as my own who I became guardian to when she and my oldest daughter were in high school together. I know that no matter what foundation my husband and I build for our children they each have freewill and their own unique set of life circumstances and personalities. However, when it comes to certain lifestyles the Bible is still the truth. It isn't that we turn our backs on our loved ones and shun them because that isn't biblical either, but we do need to speak truth into their lives and take a stand for what it means.

When one of my young adult girls asked me if I would ever disown them if they came out the closet, I was able to let her know that first of all there is no closet in homosexuality because it has been around before texting, skinny jeans and even before Jesus came to earth. Then, I let her know that nothing would keep me from loving either of them. When it came down to it my child wanted confirmation that she would never be separated from my love based on her choices. This touched me deeply as it reminded me of myself when I thought I had really messed up and didn't know if God would forgive me again.

I suppose she saw this happen in a friend's life. It hurt her to see that his family rejected him when he became open about his lifestyle. Many times, we leave ourselves wide open, and as emotional people, we may become attached to sin because we are vulnerable during certain seasons of life. Yet, I agreed that there might be people born predisposed with an attraction to the same sex just as there are people born with addictive person-alities, while others maybe prone to anger, and so on. In other words, we are born with sinful natures. Because we possess feelings and sinful natures does not make them moral. Every desire, feeling and nature has to come before God. If it is not pleasing to God, then we must reject it. With His help, we will be able to have the desire and power to live in His will. Like my daughter's friend, I recently had a close friend call me to confide in me. She sounded excited when she called to tell me, "God wants me to be happy so I'm going to do what makes me feel good." This comment was in reference to her leaving her husband and moving her female lover into the home she shared with her children. Unfortunately, what many of us miss is, in the Bible true happiness comes from living a God-centered life. This is found by serving Him, relying on Him, living for Him and receiving correction handed down from Him as in stated in: (Deuteronomy 33:29, Job 5:17, Psalm 127:5, Psalm 128:2, Psalm 144:15, Psalm 146:5, Proverb 3:13, Proverb 14:24, Proverb 16:20,

Proverb 28:14, Proverb 19:18, John 13:17, James 5:11, 1 Peter 3:14, 1 Peter 4:14).

If the world was perfect, we wouldn't need clothes and we certainly wouldn't need armor. We all would still be in the Garden of Eden having face-to-face communication with God and living perfect lives. However, Eve did pick the forbidden fruit and Adam stood and watched like a hapless victim. Now, most of us find the need for physical clothes and we all need spiritual armor if we want to survive as Christians in an increasingly depraved world.

Adam and Eve appeared to be the first human dressmakers. Their need for clothing stemmed from the shame of being naked (Genesis 3:7-8). They sewed fig leaves together and made aprons. Where did they get the idea for the pattern? Did it ever occur to you that the serpent who enticed them to eat the forbidden fruit had one on? Why did they still hide? Perhaps the inadequacy of their garments still caused them to feel shame.

This was the first time that fear entered the world. Adam and Eve knew something had changed. They didn't die in the sense of immediate death as the serpent told they wouldn't. At first, it would appear as if Satan was right and God was wrong, which was the very premise for their sin, unbelief. Yet, when their eyes opened, they suddenly experienced nakedness. It was the first time they felt insecure and a sense of impending doom must have set in. They must have sensed death on the horizon of their lives, as they once knew it.

When they hid, the all-knowing God knew where they were but he asked them where they were regardless. Adam and Eve hid among trees wearing their fig clothing and tried to blend into the scenery. God sees all of this and continues to call until he gets a response. This interaction set the stage of God's expectation from man. He wants us to answer his call to true repentance (Psalm 32:3-5, Psalm 38:4). Notice God never acknowledged that they were naked only they did. He only asks them who told them they were naked. In others words, God wanted them to see for themselves, that they were naked only because they thought of themselves as unprotected.

When God confronted Adam and Eve and saw them in their new clothing, He knew by their "dress" they had sinned because of the need to cover their sin. God didn't leave them to their own devices. As the mighty dressmaker, he created animal skin coats for the couple in response to their need. God was the first little black dressmaker. He created the ultimate garment that could be worn everywhere for every purpose. Whereas Adam and Eve made partial coverings that were made of material that was substandard, God's material required sacrifice. His material had to die before it adorned Adam and Eve. God made complete garments that would endure. The fig leaves would wilt and only last a day or two. The garments God created would last for years but production came at great sacrifice. These were the first garments documented that cost — a blood sacrifice symbolizing the sacrifice of Jesus' blood on the cross. The garments God created came from the pattern of his Son for the purpose of imitation. Just as we continue to create clothing based on God's design, we were also to copy Christ. Through biblical patterns, we follow scriptural models and examples. For instance, the creation of modern clothing is through using various patterns. Dress patterns are transferable to any assortment of material, cut according to the pattern and then sewn together according to the instructions.

Think of all the pictures you've even seen of Adam and Eve portrayed outside of the Garden of Eden. I've always seen pictures where the outfits looked very rough and basic. In some depictions I've viewed, the couple wore such rudimentary coverings it appeared as if they were cave men. However, just think the Bible said that God himself created the garments for Adam and Eve. God who created the universe, heaven and earth and all that is within, can you imagine him originating something sub-par for the couple to wear? Even designers like Coco Chanel intuitively aspire toward God's pattern of the greatest outfit ever made but never even come close. This pattern, this material, this holy garment cost the Father the sacrifice of his blameless Son, Jesus.

Throughout scripture, several instances leading up to the crucifixion show where our garments were of great price and one was coming who would pay the cost of forever for that little black dress. In fact, he himself would become the little black dress — the garment of ultimate sacrifice. Prior to Christ several instances lead up to this:

- The strict law is given and with that animal's blood sacrifices required of the God's people prior to Christ.

- Jacob- used the skin of animals to cover himself and deceive his father to steal his brother's birthright.

- Joseph the son of Jacob —he was betrayed by his brother's and sold into slavery used his coat of many colors to stain with animal's blood to cover the sin of their crime

Consider the times the enemy has tried to get you to compromise your faith. In my life, I saw this when prior to my second marriage I decided to live with my fiancé on a trial basis to avoid divorce. I did this as a Christian woman who kept the third seat in the center aisle of the church balcony warm every Sunday morning. In the Bible, the issue of compromise presents itself when Moses confronted hardhearted Pharaoh. After a period, Pharaoh's magicians did the same tricks that Moses did, but he couldn't do them all. Even the greatest magicians told Pharaoh this is the finger of God. This story illustrates something other than a pattern — it illustrates a principle. A principle is a general truth applicable in a variety of situations. In this portrayal, we see that there is no power that compares to God. Even though we may make the enemy out to be equal to God, he is not. The enemy is dangerous, cunning and powerful, but no match for our God who is all-knowing and has complete authority and supreme power.

"I the Lord search the heart and test the mind, to give every man according to his ways, according to the fruit of his deeds."

Memory Verse - Romans 12:2 ESV

"Do not be conformed to this world, but be transformed by the renewal of your mind, that by testing you may discern what is the will of God what is good and acceptable and perfect."

Dr. Chapter 2 Teaching Highlights

1. With repentance we're forgiven and given grace and peace, if we don't repent we're not forgiven and eventually suffer a life on earth and in eternity without peace or grace.

2. God gave us the gift of free will. He wants us to love him of our own accord. Love is action and through love, we demonstrate obedience.

3. Be selective about friends, read the Bible, allow the Holy Spirit to saturate our hearts and check our frame of mind.

4. It is clear all people are susceptible to sin when they don't hold the things of God sacred.

5. God was the first little black dressmaker. He created the ultimate garment that could be worn everywhere for every purpose. Whereas Adam and Eve made partial coverings that were made of material that was substandard, God's material required sacrifice.

1. Describe how you can be deceived by focusing on the wrong things.

2. Read the following verse and discuss.

"The Lord reigneth, he is clothed with majesty; the Lord is clothed with strength, wherewith he hath girded himself; the world also is established, that it cannot be moved" (Psalm 93:1 NKJ).

> a. What two words describe the way that the Lord is dressed?

> b. In what ways can you be clothed with majesty and clothed with strength?

3. List two or more areas you would like to mature in spiritually and tell how you will accomplish your goal.

4. Has God ever given you peace when you were worried and overwhelmed?

5. God gives us comfort, purpose and a hope for a future despite the circumstances, why is this?

Notes

How many
times do you
crawl back in
your memory
and kick your-
self for opening
up your big fat
mouth to the
worst person
ever?

Chapter 3

Defining Biblical Femininity

"Style is a simple way of saying complicated things."
—Jean Cocteau

Remember when I asked you in the very beginning of our journey why so many of us are unhappy? Indeed, we seem to be grappling with anxiety, depression and (SGA) Same Gender Attraction as never before. To address this, it's vital to turn back the imaginary pages of a biblical issue of Vogue to see how God dresses us in Biblical femininity. I believe God would have us understand that he created us biologically and spiritually to wear certain characteristics before hitting the runway of life. These characteristics depicted in the Bible are described as being relational, receptive, nurturing, and vulnerable, and having a deep desire to be beautiful in someone's eyes.

The 14th century gave birth to the term femininity, which means the act or nature of being feminine. Synonyms to feminine would be female, womanly, womanlike, lady-like and girlish. Although femininity is a characteristic that most women understand and strive for, it is becoming ambiguous in both purpose and meaning. Never mentioned in the Bible as an actual term, references to the idea of this concept clearly subsist as key to successful living for women. In order to address many of the issues we as women struggle with today, in other words the root of our contentions, it is key to define Biblical femininity. It is a way to bring us back to the basics to where it all started in the garden when God designed our first little black dress.

I often chuckle thinking about Eve's infamous chat and I know many of us could've gotten into trouble yakking it up with the fallen angel disguised as a serpent. Can you imagine just having one other person to talk to most of the time? Sure, besides Adam, Eve had God to talk to when he came through on his walks, but he mostly liked to ask questions. When the enemy presented himself to Eve, he appeared as someone she was able to speak freely with about controversial topics. It seemed like she could just let it all hang loose with her confidant. This wasn't really the case, but women crave relationships on so many levels that we're often misled. We may spill our guts to the wrong person at the wrong time because we're yearning for those connections so deeply. How many times do you crawl back in your memory and kick yourself for opening up your big fat mouth to the worst person ever?

I bet Eve really wanted some good girlfriends to dialog with so she could ask them about a new hairstyle she was wearing that Adam didn't notice. Perhaps, she felt if she said anything to God, He would just ask her if she liked how the new style looked. Maybe she felt she could really use some advice on the color scheme she arranged in one particular part of the garden she liked to call the living room — she thought it had a nice ring to it. All assumptions aside, God created Eve and knew her better than anyone else. He had company coming for Eve's enjoyment but Eve managed matters herself before this could happen. She entertained an unwanted guest into her heart and by default; he moved sin in as a permanent fixture. Proverbs 31, however, presents another portrayal of a woman who brings honor to her household through her character. It says that a woman with this type of character is hard to find, but her worth is far above jewels. In verses 11-12 the word reads, "The heart of her husband trusts in her, and he will have no lack of gain. She does him good and not evil all the days of her life." Honoring this godly, relational woman, the chapter tells us, "Her children rise up and bless her, her husband also, and he praises her, proclaiming: 'Many daughters have done nobly, but you excel them all.'" This prototype of a godly woman is one who is intentionally relational and blesses those in her life powerfully causing them to in turn, rise up and bless her (Proverbs 31:11-12).

Now let me let you in on a little secret, like many of you I've smiled and said "amen" in church whenever a pastor commended the ways of the Proverbs 31 woman. Nevertheless, if I were to be honest, for years I've wanted to scratch this woman's eyes out because not even on Mother's Day have I had my children rise up from anywhere to bless and praise me. In fact, my last Mother's Day I got into an argument with my 14-year-old at church because she didn't like where I'd chosen for us to sit, she didn't like the lighting! My six-year-old had an attitude because I didn't give her any of my communion cracker or juice. She even threw her sister's pen on the floor and refused to pick it up until I gave her the evil eye so bad I may need a new pair of bifocals.

Later that day, I had to tiptoe out of my youngest daughter's piano recital early to be able to beat my guests to my house. The problem is I had to bribe my 19-year-old into helping me prepare for the Mother's Day Brunch I was hosting at our home. My husband never did make it to church because he was too overwhelmed from fixing all of us an elaborate breakfast. In fact, this tuckered him out so badly that he fell asleep with his suit lying across the bed and the sink stacked high with pots and pans. In retrospect, I only began to relate to this prototype of a godly woman in Proverbs 31 when I let go of the measuring stick of comparison and realized that I am intentionally relational and I do bless others in my life powerfully. The caveat is my blessings may not only come from my immediate family but from outsiders. All of which has already happened. In addition, the timing of my blessing from my family may come in different forms and ways that demonstrate their appreciation for me by way of their own interpretation. Last, this all happening is in the hands of their will and I have no control over that.

When I was about twelve, my parents legally adopted their first child. About five years later, they legally adopted another child. Like clockwork, 5 years from that point, they unofficially "adopted" the last male young adult who would be engrafted into the family through spiritual adoption. We were always included in the adoption process in some way. Our parents would ask us what we thought and wanted our input. Sometimes they took our juvenile advice verbatim and other times they made their own calls, but we usually felt like we were an integral part of the family. Despite the obstacles of cultivating relationships with our brothers, we all experienced a bond with each of our siblings virtually identical to a blood relation. We played hard, fought hard, but in the end loved harder than most would with the challenges we faced.

My mother would often forget she didn't birth my two younger brothers. Sometimes she'd be swapping labor and delivery stories with her friends and would stumble over the details in her adopted son's stories only to recall she hadn't birthed them at all. In chapter 49 in Isaiah the word clearly describes the quality of nurturer in a woman, "Can a woman forget her nursing child and have no compassion on the son of her womb? Even these may forget, but I will not forget you. Behold I have inscribed you on the palms of My hands; your walls are continually before Me." This vivid passage is key to understanding the heart of God. He reveals himself as one who will never forget us to the point where he has us permanently etched on his palms. This means despite the brevity or length of our lives, how legendary or insignificant we were to the world, we matter to God (NKJV Isaiah 49:15-16).

As women, we emulate the heart of the Father unique from men because they can't be mothers. The ability to mother, to nurture even with the constraints of our bodies due to infertility, singleness or parenting by virtue of adoption, impact the distinctive design of our bodies. Our breasts serve as comforting places for babies to feed from or nestle on. Our hips ease carrying even a large child on one side and goodness knows what else on the other. The essence of who we are as women, even when we shroud it in false masculinity or lesbianism, connects us intimately to the heart of God because of our ability to reproduce and nurture by our very nature (Davis 2011).

Have you ever noticed how women will take the seed of thought and nurture it into a tree of many ideas just as her body would in creating a physical child? Our nature should be one to spur others and ourselves onto growth. Are you doing this very thing in a constructive manner? I hope so because too many times we women squander this ability as nurturers and instead stagnate growth and kill dreams, friendships and faith at its very root with the choking weeds of gossip, negativity and passivity. Surveying the word, we see examples of the capabilities of women. We also see how they're reflective of the nurturing heart of the Father (Davis 2011).

"I will comfort you there in Jerusalem as a woman comforts her child" (NLT Isaiah 66:13). "As apostles of Christ we certainly had a right to make some demands of you, but instead we were like children among you. Or we were like a mother feeding and caring for her own children" (NLT 1 Thessalonians 2:7).Proverbs 18:19 reads, "A brother offended is harder to be won than a strong city, and contentions are like the bars of a citadel." God is speaking to both men and women here. However, we women often create walls around our hearts to avoid vulnerability. I know this tactic well. I used it to prevent myself from abuse or rejection. It worked! Sadly, it didn't work for very long. No one got close enough to me to hurt me but all I had was a collection of empty relationships.

Thoughtlessly, I kept out the good things in my life that could help heal the pain I'd harbored in my heart for so long. Even though I had to be vulnerable to know people and to allow them to know me, it came with its pros and cons. You see, without people in my life to be intimately relational with there could be no healing from the past and growth toward the future. Sometimes women who've survived abuse seek out same sex relationships, as was the case with a friend I went to school with. She expressed her fears of looking attractive to men by playing down her voluptuous figure with shapeless articles of clothing. A sufferer of sexual assault I too, understood her battle. Yes, it was difficult to trust in the very concept of an identity who'd taken advantage of us as female children. The wise woman builds her house, but the foolish tears it down with her own hands" (NKJV Proverbs 14:1).

Similarly, in Genesis 30:13 the Bible describes an extreme instance of self-absorption. With horror, many of us women watched as Leah used the wrong motives to attain happiness when all Jacob really wanted was her younger, more beautiful sister, Rachel. I believe many of us can identify with Leah in so many ways because we've been vulnerable. We have wanted someone or something so bad we either contemplated compromising or did compromise who we were to get what we wanted. Often, I've wanted to reach through the pages of time to take Leah by the shoulders and shout, "Drop the mandrakes! No more of this foolishness girlfriend, just give it up. Stop having those babies, it is not going to make him love you!"

Childbearing became some sort of contest to win Jacob's love. Even after Leah went through menopause, she began having her female servants bear children for her. The first time this happens, she is so thrilled she named the child "Asher" which means "happy" or "blessed."Soon, Leah's body comes out of its state of menopause and she begins having children again without needing a surrogate. Again, her happiness is short-lived as she is clearly looking for happiness in the wrong place. As we read how this influences the family dynamics in the future, we can reason that Leah should've concentrated on the blessing of her children instead of a preoccupation with something she was unable to change.

There is a distinct and outright bitterness between Leah's children and Rachel's children. We especially see this when Joseph's demise is plotted and carried out by his half-brothers. Leah could've helped avoid this dysfunctional issue if she had nurtured a different spirit in the family. Often, the enemy will use an idol of the heart to get us off track. In this case it was something that was good but when it became an idol it became a replacement for God and hence, sinful. The takeaway from this story is when our happiness is tied to sin it will not be scripturally based and ultimately will not be pleasing to God. "To the man who pleases Him, God gives wisdom, knowledge and happiness, but to the sinner he gives the task of gathering and storing up wealth to hand it over to the one who pleases God" (Ecclesiastes 2:26).

Last, another element to defining Biblical femininity is the desire to be beautiful or perceived as such. This is huge to women, even those who appear indifferent about their appearance. Most women desperately want to the recognition of being beautiful to someone. Even if it isn't their outward appearance, women crave for others to see their heart as beautiful. Similarly, the Bible tells us that God understands this since it is our hearts that he examines and finds beautiful as seen in (1 Samuel 16:7). When the prophet Samuel was inspired by God to anoint David as king:...But the Lord said to Samuel, "Do not consider his appearance or his height, for I have rejected him. The Lord does not look at the things people look at. People look at the outward appearance, but the Lord looks at the heart."

I see this desire to be beautiful in my children all the time. Recently, my daughter collapsed at the finish line of a tough race she'd competed in during the AAU ESPN Wide World of Sports Track and Field meet. She'd run the second leg of a 400 meter relay. Sadly, the second place lead her team had fell back to third place during her sprint. When I heard she was in the medic's tent I searched for her there but didn't find her. After combing the spectator stands and outside fields, I finally found her looking for me back at the team's tent. She was still slightly out of breath with ice bags strapped to each leg and an apprehensive look on a face painted with sunburn and sweat. "Mom, you didn't say I looked great out there on the field!" She met me as quickly as she could. I noticed she heavily favored her right side and clutched my arm for support as she limped by my side. "Mom!" I was torn. I avoided the stares of some team parents burning into the side of my neck as I turned her away from the group and hugged her. "You looked beautiful out there." Is what I should have said but I didn't? I messed up the moment and tried to diplomatically tell her that she'd not run her best. Then, I proceeded to give her a generic pep talk with a few pointers on how she could improve her time. I missed my chance to dress her with validation.

Throughout the day, my daughter became more difficult and by the time we were in the car for the two and a half hour drive back home, she was throwing a temper tantrum like a toddler. I contemplated pulling off the highway and throttling her with an overpriced Mickey Mouse fan I'd purchased for her little sister. I soon got distracted at a tollbooth that took my picture after I drove off without paying the correct amount of change. The last straw was when she and her six-year-old sister began fighting over a toy. Finally, I pleaded with her to tell me what was bugging her. Sniffling she said, "You didn't tell me I looked good after I ran my race and that hurt because no one said I looked good." I tried giving her constructive criticism again then I saw her body hunched over in the rear-view and stopped mid-sentence. I saw myself in that reflection, remembering when I'd struggled along as a young professional. I recalled all the times when I longed for someone to whisper even one word of encouragement to me and all I heard was silence, or worse, criticism. I remembered those aching feelings of dejection. I got it. About eight hours late, but I got it.

I looked back at her just narrowly missing a massive truck and told her she looked great out on the track and that I was proud of her. She sat up with her shoulders thrown back and a broad smile showing a mouthful of braces. "Oh thanks mom! I love and appreciate you so much!" Then she turned to her sister and offered to play a DVD for them. The girls snuggled under a blanket sneaking handfuls of a forbidden bright orange crunchy snack and watched a movie as though the last hour had never happened. At last, a break-through. "Thank you God," I whispered choking back tears as I switched lanes and avoided eye contact with the driver of the 18-wheeler barreling past me into the night. Despite the deepening darkness, as I drove home the evening was dressed in a shroud of light.

"Can a woman forget her nursing child, And not have compassion on the son of her womb? Surely, they may forget, yet, I will not forget you. See, I have inscribed you on the palms of My hands; Your walls are continually before Me."

Memory Verse - Proverbs 31:11-12 ESV

"Her children **rise up** *and call her blessed; her* husband *also,* and he praises her.
Many women have done excellently,
but you *surpass them all."*

Dr. Chapter 3 Teaching Highlights

1. Biblical femininity is described as being relational, receptive, nurturing, vulnerable, and having a deep desire to be perceived as beautiful in someone's eyes.

2. Proverbs 31 presents a portrayal of a woman who brings honor to her household through her character.

3. When we let go of the measuring stick of comparison we are more sensitive, and we bless others in a powerful manner. In turn, we receive; blessings that may not come from the people we expect.

4. The scripture reminds us that despite how the world may try to belittle us God loves us so much that he has "inscribed you on the palms of My hands; your walls are continually before Me." (Isaiah 49).

5. The Bible is chocked full of people being vulnerable to each other and to God. However, the book of Psalm is particularly filled with some of, the most heartfelt and vulnerable cries for help.

"From the depths of despair, O LORD, I call for your help." Psalm 130:1.

"I think of God, and I moan, overwhelmed with longing for his help." Psalm 77:3.

"O God, why have you rejected us so long?" Psalm 74:1. "Rescue me from the mud; don't let me sink any deeper." Psalm 69:14.

"I am exhausted from crying for help; my throat is parched. My eyes are swollen with weeping, waiting for my God to help me. Those who hate me without cause outnumber the hairs on my head." Psalm 69:2-4.

"From the ends of the earth, I cry to you for help when my heart is overwhelmed." Psalm 61:2.

"My heart pounds in my chest. The terror of death assaults me. Fear and trembling overwhelm me, and I can't stop shaking." Psalm 55:4.

"As a deer longs for streams of water, so I long for you, O God. I thirst for God, the living God." Psalm 42:1-2.

"My heart is breaking as I remember how it used to be." Psalm 42:4.

"Why am I so discouraged? Why is my heart so sad?" Psalm 42:5.

"My heart beats wildly, my strength fails, and I am going blind." Psalm 38:10.

1. Using examples from the verses on the previous page (or others you find) explain what vulnerable looks like to you and why.

2. Read the following passage: (Isaiah 49:15-16)"Can a woman forget her nursing child, and not have compassion on the son of her womb? Surely, they may forget, yet I will not forget you. See, I have inscribed you on the palms of My hands;your walls are continually before Me."

> a. Using this verse, describe how God constantly has us on His mind despite the treatment of man and or our present circumstances.

> b. Notice that God didn't say I wrote your name on one hand but on His palms. What do you believe is the significance of this?

3. What is one particular idea you are proud of because you nurtured it and helped grow it into reality? This could be anything from an amazing recipe to the concept for a book club, business idea, or nonprofit organization.

4. Give an example of one particular idea or dream you've always had but never pursued? What happened? What's holding you back from achieving this goal?

5. Are there things in your life that limit you from God's presence? What are some ways to be on guard for disruptions and distractions that rob your time with God and His people?

6. When you face setbacks, do you find support from other believers? Why or why not? Why does the Bible tell us to bear one another's burdens?

Notes

...I let go of the
measuring stick
of comparison
and realized that
I am intentionally
relational...

Chapter 4

Little Black Dressers in the Bible

"Luxury is...to be able to take control of one's life, health, and the pursuit of happiness in a way that is joyful."
—Andre Leon Talley

Have you ever wondered what you could possibly learn from the believers written about in the Bible? I mean they're in the Bible for goodness sake! I think that beats out any person — no matter how fabulous — featured in magazines, TV shows, radio stations or any other form of social media. Many times, I've overlooked the humanness of those portrayed in the Bible. I think my eyes rolled to the back of my head a little bit whenever a pastor referenced people like David, Sarah or Esther. After more investigation into the fabric of their lives: it was the flaws within the cloth of their mistakes that really made me like them.

I appreciate that before he became king, David started as a simple shepherd with only a mere vision of becoming a soldier one day. The description of him physically is short of statute, handsome, and "ruddy" or healthy-looking. The scripture reveals that despite his compact size, David also had the heart of a warrior. He proved this by killing a bear and a lion on separate occasions with his bare hands. Alone, David prepared himself for the task of defeating the great rival antagonist of the Israelites mentally, spiritually and physically. Yet, it's clear by the reaction of his brothers and father, that they had no faith in his capabilities and openly criticized him for aspiring to such great ambition.

Secretly, I really liked this. It's a point I've always kept quiet at Bible studies, but I dug that his siblings gave him such a hard time since it's something I can relate to on a personal level. I believe David dealt with some self-doubt as well as shown when he succumbed to actually putting on the king's armor. When the time came for him to go into battle with the giant Philistine opponent, David did attempt to fit into King Saul's "dress."He soon realized the bulky armor he wasn't accustomed to wearing was more of a hindrance to him. It weighed him down and it didn't fit well. David soon knew that he'd become too fixated on fitting into something that was custom-made for someone else.

Tell me ladies, how many times have we done this? How many times have we envied some else's position in life without weighing the price of what it cost them? I know I've been guilty of this countless times. If we don't watch ourselves we'll end up bitter and envious of others while trying to fit into lives never made for us. However, David caught himself in time before making this grave mistake. He realized he had to return what belonged to King Saul and be stripped back to the "armor of light" Paul references in (Romans 13:11-12) in what seems to be a prophetic act of the putting on of Christ. In so doing, he allows God to freely flow through him. He got the fact that his "dress" wasn't literal, but that it was an attitude of faith, determination and an understanding that God is the ultimate "dressmaker." When we read the entire passage of the taking off the darkness, and the putting on the light in Romans 13 it's easy to relate it to current times:

"And do this, understanding the present time: The hour has already come for you to wake up from your slumber, because our salvation is nearer now than when we first believed. The night is nearly over; the day is almost here. So let us put aside the deeds of darkness and put on the armor of light. Let us behave decently, as in the daytime, not in carousing and drunkenness, not in sexual immorality and debauchery, not in dissension and jealousy. Rather, clothe yourselves with the Lord Jesus Christ, and do not think about how to gratify the desires of the flesh" (Romans 13:11-14).

Another figure in the Bible who believed that if God would be the one in charge of her ultimate makeover she would have to allow him to dress her with humility and wisdom was Esther. Her competitors didn't throw her off or intimidate her out of her blessing. She didn't go for the elaborate dress or accessories. She took advice and sought what would flatter her. She prepared herself and her heart before choosing what she would put on. This young Jewish orphan used prayer, fasting and wise counsel. She spent her time wisely and won the favor of others, those in positions of influence. She didn't feed into who was doing what but who could do what. She had to cast off the garments of abandonment, fear and inferiority in order to wear garments of bold confidence, integrity and righteousness. She took the time rationed to her and prepared her body, soul and mind to meet the king. She made sure her "dress" was memorable.

I just love that Esther had favor with the eunuch in charge of the women. He paid close attention to Esther's needs because she was down-to-earth and was not demanding. She didn't act as if she knew it all. In fact, the Bible tells us plainly that she asked for the eunuch's advice and he gave it to her willingly. This relationship is important. It symbolizes our relationship to God also interrelating to our interaction with Christ who acts as an intercessor on our behalf and petitions his father because of us. Many of those women awaiting their turn to visit with the king probably overlooked the importance of the eunuch just as there are those today who overlook Jesus. Most all religions will recognize God as the Godhead but many reject Christ and the concept of the Holy Trinity. We see this reoccurring pattern from the very beginning of time. Satan seeks to separate us from our Savior evident in Matthew 4, where he urged Jesus to trade in his original mission of dying on the cross for all men as the ultimate act of love. Satan knew that Jesus had come to rectify what Adam had corrupted but sought to get him off track by presenting him a seemingly easier way out. Satan promised Jesus all the kingdoms of the earth if he would just bow down and worship him.

The concept of the LBD has been around for ages. Rationally, darker colors became favored to use in mourning to display the sadness and darkness felt within. It also became a status symbol among the extremely rich as black dye was very difficult to make or purchase. Many times this color fabric was reserved for only special occasions or for extremely important banquets and festivities. During Queen Esther's day, this color was available, but only after her confirmation as queen because it was so expensive to make. The design of dress during that time would have involved a tunic with an overlay of some sort of cloak.

The queen must have taken great pains to ready herself for the king when she was to go before him on behalf of her people. The problem was he hadn't called for her in many days and coming before the king before summoned was punishable by death. I'd say Esther really had the pressure on to choose the ultimate black dress so that the king would say yes to anything that came out her mouth. It would seem Esther's life runs parallel to Coco's. They are both orphans and victims of war-torn times where people around them suffer persecution. They must use their cunning to survive and to protect their lives and the lives of those around them. They were also always in a constant state of grief whether or not anyone detected it or not. Motherless and fatherless, a certain loneliness must have permeated the fabric of their lives.

Coco knew what it meant to grieve. In multiple interviews, she talked about remembering the French women in her village wearing black to mourn their deceased. She expressed that she saw these women as a fashion statement. Gabrielle, now Coco, became the mistress of a very wealthy heir Etienne Balsam. This man introduced her to another wealthy man who she began dating. Arthur Edward "Boy" Carpel helped move her to her own apartment in Paris and financed the start of her clothing business. Yet, he went onto marry someone else. After he died in a car accident, Coco would then go onto date several men who would marry other women, yet would continue to date her. This included a Nazi War officer. When Coco Chanel died at 87 years old, she was wealthy and successful but she had never married or had children.

Another example of a little black dresser is Rebekah. Before I delve into her dress, I'd like to look at the love story of Isaac and Rebekah as an incredible journey of faith. Rebekah was humble and willing to serve others. She paid attention to her environment and went beyond everything asked of her. She did this without expecting anything. Surely, she didn't go to the well seeing a servant there with his many animals and thinking to herself "hmmm...maybe if I hook up this strange group, I'll get to marry a millionaire, and then go off to a new and exciting place where I will meet my rich handsome husband. Yes!"

Nope, these thoughts are very unlikely because of her character. She was just being the girl she always was. Note that the servant of the Lord was very purposeful in how he gave her certain gifts. After she served him at the well, he gave her a nose ring and bracelets. Later at her home after confirming whom her family was he gave her jewelry and clothing. Then he gave her brother and mother expensive gifts as well. This is symbolic of the blessing that a woman can be to those around her.

Although, we have a clear picture of the type of woman that Abraham wanted for his son, we do not have any background on what it is that Rebekah wanted. However, based on the events that occurred and her willingness to comply with this unorthodox match-maker who is nameless and referred to as Abraham's servant, we can safely assume that she'd been conjuring up images of her dream man all along and Isaac fit her taste. Once she agreed to go with the servant on blind faith, she has the added benefits of fine jewelry and clothing. Even her family flourishes from expensive gifts.

When she saw Isaac, she got off her camel and asked who he was. His presence stirred something inside of her and she allowed herself to move from her position of comfort. Many of us really need to ask the Lord and his servants who the people in our lives are, especially when we are moving closer to them. When you are too close to them, it is difficult to be discerning.

Some of us are in a position where we are unwilling to demonstrate change. Changing the position you see a person from is vital to a relationship. Prior to meeting Isaac she took her veil and covered herself. She did not let it all hang out upon their first meeting. She was modest, intriguing and worth the wait.

Based on her prior actions, someone close to Isaac had good things to say about Rebekah and how he'd come to find her and her family. It is significant that Isaac brought Rebekah to the tent of his deceased mother. Sarah was a respected woman who he held in high esteem. It displayed that he thought of Rebekah in the same way. This relationship brought him comfort.

Too many women look to be clothed or armored the wrong way or have the timing all mixed up. Immediately, many of us, after receiving Christ, want bedazzlement with all the spiritual gifts, as well as abundance in riches and favor. Yet, we want to stay the same in our hearts. We want to still have a bad attitude, throw temper tantrums when we don't get our way, act nasty to others, and blame it all on God that he doesn't bless us as he blesses others. However, like Rebekah, God wants us humble, looking how to be a blessing to others and obedient. It is after this he can trust us with the bling!

Prayer & Teaching Scripture Focus – Romans 13:11-14

"And do this, understanding the present time: The hour has already come for you to wake up from your slumber, because our salvation is nearer now than when we first believed. The night is nearly over; the day is almost here. So let us put aside the deeds of darkness and put on the armor of light. Let us behave decently, as in the daytime, not in carousing and drunkenness, not in sexual immorality and debauchery, not in dissension and jealousy. Rather, clothe yourselves with the Lord Jesus Christ, and do not think about how to gratify the desires of the flesh."

"*For if you* remain silent *at this time*, relief and deliverance
for the Jews will arise from another place,
but you and your father's family will perish.
And who knows but that you have come to your *royal position*
for such a time as this?"

Dr. Chapter 4 Teaching Highlights

1. David attempted to fit into King Saul's "dress" but he realized the bulky armor was more of a hindrance to him. If we don't catch ourselves we'll end up bitter and envious of others while trying to fit into lives never made for us. David realized he had to return what belonged to King Saul and be stripped back to the "armor of light" in what seems to be a prophetic act of the putting on of Christ.

2. In the book of Esther a young Jewish orphan used prayer, fasting, and wise counsel. Esther had to cast off the garments of abandonment, fear and inferiority in order to wear garments of bold confidence, integrity and righteousness. She took the time rationed to her and prepared her body, soul and mind to meet the king. She made sure her "dress" was memorable.

3. Abraham's servant gave Rebekah jewelry and clothing. Then he gave her brother and mother expensive gifts as well. This is symbolic of the blessing that a woman can be to those around her. When Rebekah saw Isaac, she got off her camel and asked whom he was. His presence stirred something inside of her and she allowed herself to move from her position of comfort. Changing the position from how you see a person is vital to a relationship. Prior to meeting Isaac she took her veil and covered herself. She did not let it all hang out upon their first meeting. She was modest, intriguing, and worth the wait.

1. When the time came for him to go into battle with the giant Philistine opponent, David did attempt to fit into King Saul's "dress." But, he realized the bulky armor he wasn't accustomed to wearing was more of a hindrance to him. Ever found yourself in a dressing room attempting to get into clothing that seemed beautiful but just didn't your body? How did this make you feel? Describe a time that was just the opposite.

2. How can the experiences of being unable to fit into a garment meant for someone else's body and finding the perfect fit for your body help you to understand what David went through?

3. Have you ever been too close to a person to be able to be objective regarding them? (For instance, your child received a negative report from school and you instantly jump into defense mode without even hearing from the school's side.)

4. Have you ever been too distant from a person to share common ground? (For example, do you look at the news in a one-sided manner and instantly side with a particular political party or way of thinking without hearing all the facts). How can this be dangerous?

5. In what ways can you manipulate your schedule to enjoy unhurried time with God in prayer and reading the Bible?

6. Share ways you can create a specific and calculated prayer battle-plan and follow it.

Notes

_____

_____

_____

_____

_____

_____

_____

_____

_____

_____

_____

_____

_____

_____

_____

_____

_____

_____

_____

_____

_____

_____

God
tailor-makes
our assign-
ments and
always has
just the
right role or
"dress" in
mind for us.

Chapter 5

Story of Modern Little Black Dressers

*"Only when you know who you are will you be able
to find the courage to do what drives you—
with integrity and grace."*
–Bethann Hardison

I remember enjoying the company of two girlfriends as we sat and ate bowls of sugary cereal giggling between mouthfuls not caring if milk dribbled on our chins as we talked. All the while, our children ran around the house screaming as if they were a hockey game crowd. The children seemed glad that we paid little attention to them, as we were deep in conversation. They slid on forbidden banisters, ate candy from dishes that were supposed to be too high for them to reach, and screamed louder than their legal limit. It was a great night.

That evening two of us paid special attention to our friend who was going through a rough time at work with several female colleagues. Despite the impeccable evaluation she'd just received from her boss, she fought feelings of inadequacy because of the treatment she'd experienced from her peers. Many of them openly voiced that she was too confident, didn't come to work early enough, stay late enough and should stop working from home twice a week.

As we listened and asked questions, we found that our friend's schedule had been tailor-made for her by her supervisor. We also discovered that the people making the judgments didn't know what her unique role was. She'd been hand-selected to update the entire region using advanced technology, of which she was an expert. We also found that her boss knew her well from working with her in another region but was still in the same state she'd left before he sent here to embark on this integration project.

However, this supervisor monitored her every step from afar. Because of the highly technical nature of her assignment, her boss knew exactly what she did. Every colleague judging her in the new assignment had no power to evaluate her, supervise her or educate her in anyway. Yet, our friend was beginning to question her performance based on the image people had formed of her. She considered rejecting the advantage of working from home to go into the office every day to show the other women how hard she was working. What they didn't know was her assignment often caused her to be on call 24 hours a day. Rejecting the schedule her boss had created for her would create an 80-to-90-hour workweek.

Once we discussed the situation, we were able to reassure her that she didn't need the counsel or affirmation of the women in her office because they had no real power over her assignment. She'd given them power by allowing them to manipulate her worth, emotions and view of herself to a much lower standard than she deserved. We both read the last two years of her evaluations, and we were impressed by her credentials. We'd always known she was bright and hardworking, but the evaluations said it all. It described her many accomplishments and abilities in a distinct manner. It was evident our girlfriend was a prized employee and her boss had taken every opportunity possible to point that out.

After another round of cereal, coffee and several trips to the bathroom, we found out our friend's boss had recently made a special trip to see her and had brought his wife along. This trip entailed a dinner in our friend's honor where all her colleagues were invited as he honored her with a plaque detailing her long list of accomplishments at the five-year mark of her time with the company.

All throughout this wonderful evening as we helped our friend focus on what was important I couldn't help but praise God for the understory of this situation. Just like my girlfriend, many of us all make the mistake of focusing in on those close to us. We wrongfully look at who is making the most noise and trying to show us how incompetent and inferior we are. Sadly, these same people will try to show us we're not fitting in. When in reality, God tailor-makes our assignments and always has just the right role or "dress" in mind for us. God has also given us the Bible as the life-affirming blueprint. It is the ultimate evaluation. It is confirmation that our existence is designed with purpose.

My beautiful, intelligent girlfriend had become plagued with stress, depression and anxiety because she was slowly taking off the "dress" of success made just for her. She almost traded her unique "tailor-made" dress to put on the cookie cutter dress of mediocrity worn by most of her complaining colleagues. Looking back on that evening, I can now see that each of us wore our black dress differently. With a little help from each other, we parted ways looking better spiritually. We were able to zip up a friend's dress for it to fit with confidence. We each pulled up any loose straps of judgment and tucked them back into their rightful places. Finally, we were able to adorn our spirits with the diamonds of friendship.

Some of my favorite people to talk to are my mother and my mother-in-law. They are filled with vibrant memories of growing up and raising their families. Their lives are treasure chests of wisdom that I try to borrow from as much as I possibly can. While they had incredibly different experiences being from different countries, traditions, and backgrounds, there are things about them that are strikingly similar and I can only attribute this to their devoted lives to the re-born again Christian faith.

The sayings of a Jamaican are rich, diverse and impactful. A few I will share with you that I recall my mother saying throughout my life. I will try my best to relate it to our lives as it applies to us now as we battle being overwhelmed. Therefore, when I ask you to, please close your eyes, and visualize a few scenarios.

(Close your eyes and imagine a steaming bowl of rice right out of the pot. You grab your fork and prepare to eat when you hear these words and open your eyes...) Don't eat rice when it's hot — when feeling overwhelmed and faced with a crisis of any sort, don't react immediately. Give the situation a waiting period for things to cool down before being responsive.

(Close your eyes and imagine an enormous ant mound by your feet, you raise your foot and stomp on the giant ants one by one. Now open your eyes and listen...) If you mash ants you find his guts — people reveal their true colors and what is really inside them when pressure is applied to their lives and when hard times happen.

(Close your eyes and imagine it's nighttime and the moon is shining large, glossy, and bright into your window. Now open your eyes and hear this saying...) The older the moon, the brighter it shines — an older person shines wisely with the knowledge of experience and having been where many haven't traveled.

(Close your eyes and imagine a sunny day sitting beside a glistening, deep river with various stones at the very bottom. Now open them and hear this ...) Rock-stones on the river bottom don't know the sun is hot — sheltered people don't know true hardships or troubles.

My mother in law loves telling stories of her adventures as a passenger in the family car her deceased husband drove. A victim of the time she grew up in, it wasn't customary for women to learn how to drive, especially if they were proper married women. She expressed regret regarding not learning to drive but learned to develop a true appreciation for a safe driver. In fact, she even learned to read maps and all the road signs so she could always be of assistance. As her husband's hearing issues escalated into complete deafness, she desperately tried to come up with improved ways to keep them safe on the road. She even developed a system of large hand held signs that said things like: danger, slow-down, speed up, turn right, turn left, and stop! However, one thing she learned the hard way is it's detrimental to startle a deaf person at the wheel so she was very careful as to how she approached her skittish husband. One day as she settled into the passenger seat and habitually prayed earnestly for safety, she kept hearing these words — "Would you know how to turn off this car if you had to?" She finally composed herself and calculated what she'd always observed and decided she would know how to turn off the car if she had to. No sooner had she done this, the car was hit and pushed into an intersection. To her horror, her husband was passed out and slumped over the wheel. Without batting an eyelash, she reached over and turned off the racing engine avoiding a worse dilemma than the initial accident had caused effectively saving both their lives and perhaps the lives of others.

What am I telling you when I share a few colorful Caribbean sayings? What am I really saying when I tell this story of a wife and her deaf husband? I'm sharing practical steps and truths we can all use to prepare to be overwhelmed. Why? Because eventually there will come a time when we are faced with being burdened, it's just a matter of when. A wise woman will pay attention to sayings meant to instruct. A wise woman will pay attention to stories of a wife listening to a still small voice asking her if she's prepared to meet the challenge of the moment. You see moments make up hours, hours make up days, days make up years and years make up a life! Therefore, if we live our moments right we live our lives right.

Key Scriptures to remember:

But the LORD watches over those who fear him, those who rely on his unfailing love (Psalm 33:18).

Teach them to obey everything that I have taught you, and I will be with you always, even until the end of this age (Matthew 28:20).

The LORD is fighting for you! So be still (Exodus 14:14).

Peace I leave with you. My peace I give to you. I do not give to you as the world gives. Your heart must not be troubled or fearful (John 14:27).

Notes

_____

_____

_____

_____

_____

_____

_____

_____

_____

_____

_____

_____

_____

_____

_____

_____

_____

_____

_____

_____

_____

_____

"We are hard pressed on every side, but not crushed; perplexed, but not in despair; persecuted, but not abandoned; struck down, but   not destroyed."

"Do not lie to each other,

since you have taken off your old self *with its practices and have* put on the new self, *which is being renewed in knowledge in the* image of its Creator. "

Chapter 5 Teaching Highlights

1. Many of us all make the mistake of focusing in on those close to us. We wrongfully look at who is making the most noise and trying to show us how incompetent and inferior we are. Sadly, these same people will try to show us we're not fitting in.

2. In reality God tailor-makes our assignments and always has just the right role or "dress" in mind for us.

3. To hear God's voice we need to read the word and be in prayer but allow time to listen.

4. Above all, God is interested in our obedience.

5. God sent us the Holy Spirit to lead us and help us.

1. Describe in your own words your personal experience with trials of being deceived and or misled by people.

2. In reality God tailor-makes our assignments and always has just the right role or "dress of success" in mind for us. The Bible tells us in Philippians 4:6, "Do not be anxious about anything, but in every situation, by prayer and petition, with thanksgiving, present your requests to God." How can you effectively avoid the pitfalls of anxiety, stress, and depression by "covering yourself" with this scripture?

3. Imagine going through the expense and trouble of getting a custom-made dress then trading it in for a cheaply made cookie cutter dress of mediocrity worn by your competitors. Why would women trade in their unique gifts for what everyone else has?

4. Have you ever been caught up into wanting to fit in so much that you just stopped being unique? What is it about you that you believe you've lost? How can you get that tailor-made girl back, in other words explain how you can purposely nurture your unique person with unique gifts to be a blessing to God and others?

5. What are some things that God has revealed to you about Himself?

6. What are some things that God has revealed to you about yourself?

Notes

I fought
with truth,
tap-danced
with it and
even sent
it to call
waiting.

Chapter 6

A Visit With the Tailor
Seeking God for the Truth

"I design for the woman I wanted to be,
the woman I used to be and to some degree,
the woman I'm still a little piece of."
- Diane Von Furstenberg

Have you ever struggled and lost the battle when asked to tell the truth? Well my friend, you are in good company if you are being honest right now. There have been times I'm not very proud of where I've been frugal with the truth, yes, just down-right stingy. According to statics, it's reported that on average people are lied to about 200 times a day. After hearing that particular report, I really tried to pay attention to what was leaving my brain and coming out of my mouth. According to an article: 10 Research Findings About Deception That Will Blow Your Mind (Blog post for "Lie spotting: Proven Techniques to Detect Deception," Pamela Meyer, St. Martin's Press 2010) thousands of controlled scientific studies revealed findings that can be summarized in several the following key points:

Humans are lied to as many as 200 times a day.

Humans detect lies with only 54% accuracy.

Between 75% and 82% of lies go undetected.

Of the lies we tell, 25% are for someone else's sake.

Gorillas, fish, birds and even orchids engage in deception.

Avoiding eye contact is the most presumed sign of lying around the world—even though it's false.

Law enforcement officials—including FBI agents, customs agents and judges— performed no better than the average person in detecting deception.

One in six juries reaches an incorrect verdict.

Training can improve a person's lie detection ability by 25-50%.

(http://liespotting.com/2010/06/10-research-findings-about-deception-that-will-blow-your-mind/)

There are times when I don't want to share my opinion on anyone's hairstyle, outfit, new furniture, weight, etc., because being honest means I may not have any friends. What do we do in these situations? I'll tell you what I began to do and that was to examine how Jesus handled conversations with people. I realized that he handled them very differently according to what was in their hearts. When people he conversed with were arrogant and self-righteous, he gave them the law and pointed out their hypocrisy. Yet when he sensed people genuinely seeking after truth, he knew that they were open to Him. He asked pointed questions in a purposeful manner. He also established relational environments before he attempted to speak into someone's life.

To do this he would do three things. First, he would create an opportunity for relationship by allowing people to talk about themselves. Most often people seem to enjoy having the focus on themselves in a conversation. For me this is an important application because it's a great way to remove the spotlight from self and shine it on others. Next, Jesus would speak truth lovingly. This method convicted people of the sin in their lives in a way that caused them to come to their own realization. Finally,

Jesus would reveal himself to people giving them the opportunity to either accept him or reject him.

This pattern does work if we're patient and sensitive to the Holy Spirit. I've learned over time when I sense push back from people during a conversation about spiritual things to just stop. If possible, I continue by finding common ground, which has now become almost effortless for me. I then continue the discussion from an earthly perspective. I can find anything in common with anyone and I think of it as a divine gift! My family would disagree because it has caused us to spend much more time anywhere we go as I jibber-jabber with every Pam, Chuck and Sally about Lord-only-knows-what.

I had a cousin who noticed this incredible gift and embarrassed me in front of a large group. She said, "I've never seen anything thing like this before, you always seem to have something in common with someone." I tried to hide it but my feelings were hurt because her observation made me seem insincere. Looking back, I can see why my cousin came to this conclusion. Her style of forging relationships is different from mine. She openly states that she aims to weed out as many people from her life as possible. As many times as I've been hurt in friendship, this attitude could be a wise protective measure. However, not only am I wired differently but I am convinced that one of the primary purposes of a Christian is to share the gospel with others. I am not in the position to save anyone, but I can choose to be a bridge instead of a stumbling stone. The rest is up to God and that person's personal choice. The Bible tells us in John 6:44 that "No one can come to me unless the Father who sent me draws them, and I will raise them up at the last day." In essence, God has the ability to draw people to him by permission of their free will for them to accept what you have to say.

When I depend on God's ability to draw people through me I find it helps me in the way I interact with others even when not discussing the gospel. For example, if my oldest daughter asked me if I thought, her hot-pink streak was pretty I would say. "What do you think when you look in the mirror? Do you

like what you see? If you like what you see then I'm all for that."
Alternatively, if my six-year-old asked me if I thought the draw-
ing she configured in all blue-crayon looked like me I would
say, "Do you think it looks like me? Do you think people would
recognize this wonderfully creative picture of mommy? Maybe
we can have fun testing it out — what do you think about that?"

Then, there are the more serious issues like when a girlfriend calls you up to ask your true feelings about her husband
who she suspects is having an affair. Do you confess that you've
been afraid to tell her of your suspicions because of how she may
react? Do you share with her that your husband saw hers at a
shopping outlet 40 miles from his house with his mistress. How
truthful do you think you could be with another friend who con-
fesses she's been keeping an extra-marital secret? The catch is
she wants you to keep it a secret as if you're on an episode of The
Real Housewives instead of women behaving as if they really
were God-fearing.

I've been in every single one of these situations and they
were tough. I fought with truth, tap-danced with it, ignored it
and even sent it to call waiting. Ultimately, I had to take a long,
hard look at my own heart to be able to speak truth into anyone's
life. Like with my friend Kim who knew her husband was having
an affair. She was calling me for validation. It was unnecessary
for me to bring up her husband's dirt because Kim had finally
got to the point where she wanted to deal with the issue instead
of pretending it wasn't happening.

How about when your friend stops by for a visit but the two
of you can barely get a word in edgewise because her three-year-
old is either screaming or climbing to the top of your pantry to
get to the cookies you thought you hid. When she cuts the visit
short and whines that it's because Ben is so smart that it's hard
for him to behave in such traditional environments, do you agree
with her and get them out the door as quickly as possible before
something else breaks, or do you speak the truth in love? What
do you do? You do what Jesus did. He chose his words and timing wisely. My mother has a saying she got from her mother that

I mentioned, "Don't eat rice when it's too hot."In other words, in the heat of emotions don't add more heat with inflammatory words. In Jesus' teaching he sought to display the difference between seeing and blindness from a spiritual standpoint. Jesus' wisdom teaching points to the world of conventional wisdom as a world of blindness. His aphorisms and parables invite us to see differently.

When we read Luke 7:29-35 we see Jesus clarifying his role as wisdom itself: "All the people, even the tax collectors, when they heard Jesus' words, acknowledged that God's way was right, because they had been baptized by John. But the Pharisees and the experts in the law rejected God's purpose for themselves, because they had not been baptized by John.

"Jesus went on to say, "To what, then, can I compare the people of this generation? What are they like? They are like children sitting in the marketplace and calling out to each other: 'We played the pipe for you, and you did not dance; we sang a dirge, and you did not cry.'

"For John the Baptist came neither eating bread nor drinking wine, and you say, 'He has a demon.' The Son of Man came eating and drinking, and you say, 'Here is a glutton and a drunkard, a friend of tax collectors and sinners.' But wisdom is proved right by all her children."

This scripture shows us that Jesus observed the words, behavior and practices of the religious people and the people who received his teaching openly. He pointed out that his "children" were his accomplishments. When we read between the lines, we see that through them, he was justified and the very sinners that the religious folks condemned him for hanging out with were the ones doing the will and service of God. We can see a pattern in the ministry of disciple training that Jesus carried on. He did not try to reach all the masses with the gospel. Even if He had wanted to, the task would be too big. Rather He concentrated on a few selected ordinary men, who were "with Him" and to whom He gave both verbal instruction and a constant example — preparing them though their time with Him to do the same. A similar method of discipleship is practiced by the early churches in the book of Acts.

Biblical principles help us bridge the application gap between then and now. The circumstances of the biblical context may be different from our own, but the principle is the same. A principle is a truth, method or rule adopted as the basis for action or conduct. It is a general truth composed of other subordinate truths. "Subordinate" truths relate to the general truth. A biblical principle is a spiritual truth taught in scripture. Such principles often incorporate additional subordinate principles, which apply to many different situations. For example, one biblical principle taught by Jesus is "Give and ye shall receive." Its subordinate truths apply to giving money, material goods, friendship, etc. In each of these, spiritual benefits received are because of the act of giving. "God so loved the world that he gave his one and only Son, that whoever believes in him shall not perish but have eternal life"(John 3:16).Unfortunately, when we create our own value systems and religious laws apart from God we pattern a false standard of measurement. Once we begin to teach as biblical doctrine things that are nothing but commandments of men, Jesus warns us: "But in vain they do worship me, teaching for doctrines the commandments of men" (ESV Matthew 15:9).

"No one can come to me unless the Father who sent me draws them, and I will raise them up at the last day."

Memory Verse - John 3:16

"God so *loved* the world that he gave his one and *only* Son, that whoever believes in him shall not perish but have eternal life."

Dr. ✂ Chapter 6 Teaching Highlights

1. Christ gave us the greatest pattern for developing relationships. He asked pointed questions in a purposeful manner. Also, he established relational environments before he attempted to speak into someone's life.

2. First, he would create an opportunity for relationship by allowing people to talk about them. Most often people seem to enjoy having the focus on them.

3. Next, he would speak truth in love convicting people of the sin in their lives in a manner, which caused them to come to their own realization. Finally, he would reveal himself to people giving them the opportunity to either accept him or reject him.

1. What are some questions you can ask people to show an interest in them and build rapport?

2. How do you go about discussing difficult subjects with loved ones? Does your approach usually work? Why, or why not?

3. Talk about realistic ways to have a conversation with someone who has given you push-back regarding the gospel message. The Bible tells us in John 6:44 that "No one can come to me unless the Father who sent me draws them, and I will raise them up at the last day." In essence, God has the ability to draw people to him by permission of their free will for them to accept what you have to say.

4. Describe how your invitation to the gospel could be less intimidating to you with the knowledge that you aren't responsible for giving them salvation just leading them in the right direction.

5. Do you spend more time on what happens on your exterior or interior?

6. What do you base an assessment of a person on? Is it physical appearance or personality or a mixture of both?

Notes

_____

_____

_____

_____

_____

_____

_____

_____

_____

_____

_____

_____

_____

_____

_____

_____

_____

_____

_____

_____

_____

_____

The
ultimate
definition of
a woman is
in the hidden
person of
the heart.

Chapter 7

Affording for the Authentic Accessories

"Style is a way to say who you are
without having to speak."
– Rachel Zoe

Why the accessories, or spiritual assets,matter is they are the "bling" that we have when we stand before the presence of God. Our motives and how they flesh out into action is how we as women must find worth and identity in who we are in Christ. When it comes to accessories or spiritual assets, they are attributes that are universal and deemed good and desirable qualities to possess by most religious groups, cultures and communities. Ironically, the list of biblically based bling I'm sharing with you I retrieved from a secular site of The Community Tool Box of the Work Group for Community Health and Development at the University of Kansas.

- Being charitable toward others.
- Being compassionate.
- Forgiveness and reconciliation.
- Appreciation and gratitude.
- Spreading hope.
- Sharing hospitality.
- Practicing humility.
- Advocating for justice.
- Patience: Enduring trials.
- Showing tolerance and acceptance.

The attributes Christ finds precious is described in 1 Peter 3:3-6,which says, "Your adornment must not be merely external — braiding the hair, and wearing gold jewelry, or putting on dresses; but let it be the hidden person of the heart, with the imperishable quality of a gentle and quiet spirit, which is precious in the sight of God. For in this way in former times the holy women also, who hoped in God, used to adorn themselves, being submissive to their own husbands; just as Sarah obeyed Abraham, calling him lord, and you have become her children if you do what is right without being frightened by any fear."

Now, I am that woman who actually rolled her eyes and sighed when I first heard that passage. I said, "Really Sarah? Who are you kidding? You had to be one of the most defiant, conniving wives in the B-i-b-l-e!" I mean, is it just me or do people just not read their Bibles anymore. You're not fooling me sister!" Yes, I said all of this, at the top of my lungs, proudly. I read when Sarah gave her handmaid to Abraham because she was so very tired of waiting on God to provide her with a child. I read about Sarah then tossing her handmaiden out of the house after Haggai got on her high horse after having Abraham's son and started acting up even after Sarah conceived a son as well. The entire time it just seemed like Abraham was right alongside Sarah like a love struck puppy going along with all of her plans. Just because she threw around the word Lord when it came to her husband certainly didn't mean she really respected him, right? More on that in just a bit, I'd like to get back to accessorizing.

There is nothing evil about wearing make-up, nice dresses, braiding the hair or wearing gold jewelry. In fact, Ezekiel 16:1-19 God metaphorically describes himself giving Israel jewelry and nice clothing. Making outward appearance the sole objective and goal to define womanhood or to find worth in is how many of us go wrong. To believe that womanhood primarily depends upon outer appearance is lacking in biblical principles because the Bible states that anything relating to our character relates to the state of our heart. 1 Samuel 16:7 says, "But the LORD said to Samuel, 'Do not look at his appearance or at the height of his stature, because I have rejected him; for God sees not as man sees, for man looks at the outward appearance, but the Lord looks at the heart.' " Women frequently fall into the trap of thinking that they will be better or more valuable if they look better, which they measure based upon what the society says is beautiful at the time. Though husbands certainly should appreciate their wives' outward beauty, form and appearance (Song of Solomon 1:15), the ultimate definition of a woman is in the hidden person of the heart (Proverbs 31:30). God wants to see a gentle and quiet spirit, one that respects God and her husband, not in a fearful dread but in a peaceful, secure rest and trust.

A godly woman is a comfort and a companion, one whom a godly husband can trust and find delight in (Proverbs 31:11). Her tenderness and peacefulness is the adornment, which God says, is definitive of a woman of God. Women should dress to embellish their beauty, and they have the right biblically to take care of themselves outwardly. Outward beauty is not evil in and of itself, and neither is having a pleasant, elegant personality. What the Bible does condemns preoccupation with the external because it is vain, and it condemns charm that is deceitful, seductive and manipulative because it's deemed as devilish, evil, ungodly and riddled with lies. In God's view, the woman who fears the Lord is to be praised (Proverbs 31:30).

We girls need to come to see that godliness is the ultimate measure of a woman. First Timothy 2:9-10 says, "Likewise, I want women to adorn themselves with proper clothing, modestly and discreetly, not with braided hair and gold or pearls or costly garments, but rather by means of good works, as is proper for women making a claim to godliness." In other words, our true womanhood isn't found trying to see how many men we can get to check out our goods. Of course, we should look and smell good. I love great fashion—designer perfume—shoes, bags, and girlfriend believe me when I say I could go on for hours about this stuff! However, the true point here is we shouldn't be trying to seduce others with the outward but more so with our godliness.

Pastor and author Terry M. Crist wrote in a 2002 issue of Charisma Magazine in the article "Equally Redeemed From the Fall":

"God gave Eve to Adam because she completed him. She brought a unique perspective to their partnership that Adam would never have had otherwise. The same is true for men and women today. Women bring to leadership in the home, the workplace and the church what Eve brought to leadership in the Garden: grace, vulnerability and beauty, yes; but also eyes that interpret behavior, ears attuned to pain, hearts that are nurturing and resolved, courageous curiosity and insight that transcends the limitations of the male perspective. God never intended for the woman to be relegated to the sidelines while the male of the species fulfilled the dominion mandate. Women are not designed to be spectators or competitors with men; they are designed to be facilitators of the grace of life alongside men."

Like the song "It's a Man's, Man's, Man's World" (King 1966) by James Brown and Betty Jean Newsome recorded on February 16, 1966 in a New York studio and released it as a single later that year, our lives as women are constantly lived in comparison, competition and parallel to that of a man. The song's unique quality was that it was written like a sermon. The song appeared to say one thing but really meant another. This helped it reach No. 1 on the Billboard Rhythm & Blues Charts as well as No. 8 on the Billboard Hot 100. The song lists man's life enhancing inventions, but the singer admits he would be nothing without a woman. Brown embellished the fervent ballad from lyrics written by Betty Newsome. Her words were originally from the Bible and her observations of some of her ex-boyfriends, including the Godfather of Soul himself. Betty had an intuitive grip on the over encompassing gospel message better than many churchgoers. It's clear from the lyrics that she understood God's special calling on a women's life according to scripture, "But when the set time had fully come, God sent his Son, born of a woman, born under the law" (Galatians 4:4).

Now finally, back to our friend and sister Sarah, remember when I posed the question relating to her sincerity in calling Abraham Lord? The Bible clearly refers back to Sarah with all of her downfalls as a woman to emulate. There were excellent qualities of character that God wants us to pay close attention. You see, I believe that despite Abraham's own shortcomings and, often deceptive, behavior she still maintained a certain level of respect for his person and ultimately the promises that God made to them. I believe the ultimate act of selflessness that Sarah made was to allow Abraham to sacrifice her precious son on the altar as a clear indication that they placed nothing above the worship of God. She was clearly strong-willed but chose God's will during this turning point.

In the times in which Sarah lived, her barren state could have cost her the marriage she obviously valued. Abraham chose to love Sarah despite her inability to provide him with a son the traditional way. He clung fast to the promises from God that he and Sarah would be the parents of many generations to come. It's just that he couldn't fathom how it would happen given his particular situation. It appeared as if he allowed Sarah to take the lead in creating an opportunity to give him an heir. However, Abraham's error was similar to Sarah's in that they were looking at their situation from a carnal point of view. They realized that they were dealing with infertility issues and they were advancing in age. Sarah knew the type of husband that God had blessed her with and affirmed this openly, which is the reason she's praised for the highly adorned and favored woman she is to all of us.

There is also something unique about Sarah that sets her apart from every woman ever mentioned in the Bible. She is the only woman whose name was changed by God. She was first called Sarai—meaning "my princess"—but God changed her name to Sarah—signifying "princess" to all (Soncino

Commentary, comments on Genesis 17:15).But why did this name change occur? God explains this in detail in verse 16: "And I will bless her and also give you [Abraham] a son by her; then I will bless her, and she shall be a mother of nations; kings of peoples shall be from her."

Note that God said to Isaac in Genesis 26:3-4: "Dwell in this land, and I will be with you and bless you; for to you and your descendants I give all these lands, and I will perform the oath which I swore to Abraham your father. And I will make your descendants multiply as the stars of heaven; I will give to your descendants all these lands; and in your seed all the nations of the earth shall be blessed."

Also in (NLT Galatians 4:22-26) God clarifies even further: "The Scriptures say that Abraham had two sons, one from his slave wife, and one from his freeborn wife. The son of the slave wife was born in a human attempt to bring about the fulfillment of God's promise. But the son of the freeborn wife was born as God's own fulfillment of his promise. These two women serve as an illustration of God's two covenants. The first woman, Hagar, represents Mount Sinai where people received the law that enslaved them. And now Jerusalem is just like Mount Sinai in Arabia because she and her children live in slavery to the law. But the other woman, Sarah, represents the heavenly Jerusalem. She is the free woman, and she is our mother." That promised Seed was Jesus Christ! (Life, Hope & Truth Magazine, John Foster).

Prayer & Teaching Scripture Focus – 1 Peter 3:3-6

"Your adornment must not be merely external — braiding the hair, and wearing gold jewelry, or putting on dresses; but let it be the hidden person of the heart, with the imperishable quality of a gentle and quiet spirit, which is precious in the sight of God. For in this way in former times the holy women also, who hoped in God, used to adorn themselves, being submissive to their own husbands; just as Sarah obeyed Abraham, calling him lord, and you have become her children if you do what is right without being frightened by any fear."

But the Lord said to Samuel,

"*Do not look at his appearance*

or at the height of his stature, because I have rejected him;

for God sees not as man sees, *for man looks at the outward appearance,* but the LORD looks at the heart.'

Do not lie to each other, since you have taken off your old self with its practices and have put on the ***new self***, which is being renewed in knowledge in the image of its Creator."

Dr. Chapter 7 Teaching Highlights

1. God wants to see a gentle and quiet spirit, one that respects God and her husband, not in a fearful dread but in a peaceful, secure rest and trust.

2. The Bible condemns preoccupation with the external because it is vain, and it condemns charm that is deceitful, seductive, and manipulative because it's deemed as devilish, evil, ungodly, and riddled with lies.

3. We shouldn't be trying to seduce others with the outward but more so with our godliness.

4. God gave Eve to Adam because she completed him. She brought a unique perspective to their partnership that Adam would never have had otherwise.

1. Using 1 Samuel 16:7 as a guide, describe the dangers of judging a person primarily by their outward appearance, then discuss some practical measures you can take to ensure that you judge all people by their heart.

2. The accessories or spiritual assets matter because they are the "bling" that we have when we stand before the presence of God. Our motives and how they flesh out into action is how we as women must find worth and identity in who we are in Christ. Describe how you've exercised obedience in each of the following areas and then how you'd like to grow.

    a. Being charitable toward others
    b. Being compassionate
    c. Forgiving and reconciling
    d. Appreciating and having gratitude
    e. Spreading hope
    f. Sharing hospitality
    g. Practicing humility
    h. Advocating for justice
    i. Being Patient: Enduring trials
    j. Showing tolerance and acceptance

Notes

We each
have an
inheritance
in the
purpose
and plan
of God.

Chapter 8

Not Comparing Our Dress to Others

"Fashion is not something that exists in dresses only.
Fashion is in the sky, in the street;
fashion has to do with ideas,
the way we live, what is happening."
- Coco Chanel

Have you ever seen those magazine articles showing celebrities in the same dress then voting on who looks better in it? I've seen plenty of these features and just knew I'd figured out who would be voted best-dressed only to find out I was wrong. I've often wondered how they chose who looked better because I disagreed with their opinion so much. This same thing happens when we look at the lives of others through our own-tunneled vision. We may envy the way the way others look in the "dress" of their lives completely ignorant of how their lives really are.

Perhaps there is someone we know who appears to have it all or rather everything we wish we did but do not. This is because we are looking at things from our perspective. The people we envy may have washboard abs, a mansion filled with expensive furniture, perfect children, and an accomplished adoring husband. When you get their Christmas cards you may find yourself feeling like you just don't measure up and rather than putting their card on the mantle you'd much prefer ripping their matching sweaters up into red and green confetti.

The Bible says, "You will keep him in perfect peace, whose

mind is stayed on You, because he trusts in You" (NKJV Isaiah 26:3). Yet, do our minds stray instead of stay on God and we find ourselves smirking when that same family falls apart a year or two later? Perhaps the parents get divorced, they lose their riches, and the children wind up on drugs hence drop out of the Ivy-league schools where they had scholarships. Does watching the demise of others bring a certain satisfaction to our own lives? In such instances, do we smugly pat down the "dress" of our own lives and admit that we aren't looking half-bad after all? The Bible warns us to guard our hearts against this sort of thinking. We need to give our hearts a daily check-up, watching for idols that rear up like weeds and pull them out by the roots. God doesn't judge us for our success but does hold us accountable for our faithfulness. Therefore, it's vital to live godly lives, be good examples of Jesus and share the gospel with others. For the believer, the Bible is a handbook for living and helps us with these very things by having God examine our hearts: "Search me, O God, and know my heart; test me and know my anxious thoughts. Point out anything in me that offends You, and lead me along the path of everlasting life" (NLT Psalms 139:23-24).

Have you ever found yourself in a place of resentment instead of contentment for the good taking place in people's lives? I've struggled with this at times. When I distinctively felt God calling me to pray for certain people, I was suddenly tongue-tied and forgetful. I'll admit I didn't want to pray for them because I felt like they were already doing great so why waste my precious efforts when I could be praying for myself! Yet, God kept pressing me to pray for their protection and blessing. This really hit home in one particular instance with a family I'd idolized for years. They were postcard perfect from the outside looking in. Even those of us who were fairly close to them never detected anything wrong. They were the worship leaders at our church and each of their children displayed the same giftedness in music, athletics and academics as their parents. I learned so much from their examples as parents and Christians. I was in a small group that met in their home and attended with my (then) husband and small children.

I'll never forget the Friday evening I sat next to the abusive and manipulative man I'd married making sure not to let my thighs so much as touch his. Alongside us were five other couples seated on a massive sectional. During prayer, I was the only one with my eyes open because I wanted to take in everything that I didn't have myself. I glared at each happy couple praying, listened to their perfect children play while mine whined and cried in the next room, skimmed the behavior chart I wish I'd made for my family, looked at the perfectly cooked food waiting, and got madder. The perfectly baked Bundt cake centered on the kitchen counter propelled my anger from hot to boiling. I prided myself on being a good cook but this cake showcased under a sparkling glass dome had the hand of a genius on it. My anger ended in tears that ran down my face in secret twin trails as I wiped them away just as quickly as they came. When prayer was over I went back to polite conversation and smiles but something on the inside had shifted. I made sure my family left the gathering before dessert was served by making some excuse about not feeling well but I deep down inside I didn't want to be tempted to take even a bite of that cake.

It wasn't long after that incident that my marriage unraveled and I was a single mom. This family became vital to me as I leaned on them for spiritual guidance and babysitting. I can't say enough about the steadfast love they poured out on all of us when I dealt with guilt from subjecting my oldest daughter to the abuse she'd suffered at the hands of my ex-husband. This helped me to avoid being a victim by being accountable for my mistakes and letting the rest go. Their openness helped heal the fears I had that I'd never attract a godly husband who'd love me and accept my children as his own. I was able to prevent myself from being paralyzed by fear. This couple encouraged me to stay in church leadership when I felt unworthy to serve, and that experience allowed me to maximize the difficult situation I went through. I truly came to idolize them as a family and I never thought of this as wrong. When I met the man I'm married to now they were some of the first friends I wanted him to meet. He was impressed with them too but my obsession became concerning to my husband when I often referred to them as the ideal family. He gently explained how unhealthy he believed it was to put people on pedestals and that we needed to work toward making our own blended family better instead of focusing on the idea of theirs.

A few months later, I received a call from the wife of the very family I'd idolized. Choking back tears my friend explained she'd be moving out of state as soon as the divorce was final with her husband of 22 years. It turns out he'd become distant and violent to her and her children and she couldn't live the terrible secret she'd been living for the past several months. Immediately after that conversation, I felt convicted. I wondered if my friend's situation would've turned out differently if people like me had been praying for her rather than envying her. I thought of all the times this family had poured into my life by being godly role models but I never reciprocated their goodness in prayer for them because I didn't feel they needed it. This incident convinced me that families appearing to "have it all" are just as vulnerable to the enemy's attacks as any other family. In fact, we all need others to shine and be examples just as much as they need the support and prayers of fellow believers.

Shortly after our talk, I went to visit my girlfriend. As I walked through the marble corridors, there was a stillness to the once bustling home I'd not noticed before. As we sat at her kitchen table drinking coffee, she remarked how empty the home had become. Her husband had moved out during the divorce and two of her four children had left to attend college. There were packing boxes everywhere and it was clear that the remaining household would be moving soon. Leaving her that day was hard because the distance and changes placed an uncertainty on everything, including our friendship. As I walked to the door, something familiar shoved in a corner caught my eye. There sat the perfect cake in a cardboard box. It was the same cake I'd envied a few years ago in a couples Bible study. Seeing the bewilderment on my face as I examined the cake, my friend laughed and pulled the heavy glass top off the cake. She told me to touch it. When I did touch what looked like an expert icing job, it was rock hard. She continued to laugh and said, "Looks like my fake cake got you too. It fools everyone!" I found out the cake was actually a candle made to look and smell exactly like a cinnamon Bundt cake!

I know from personal experience that pride results in all manifestations of sin in my life. It often starts small, so small I may not even notice it's an issue. Not only can pride result in comparing myself to others, which leads to envy, but it can result in being victimized and paralyzed, as opposed to being maximized. When I don't acknowledge that God is with me in every situation, I'm often paralyzed with fear. This leads to help-lessness. It renders me ineffective and causes me to be unable to live in the present. However even when tragedy strikes, God is still with us. To be spiritually paralyzed, is to have the right equipment but you can't use it.

A victim mentality comes in quickly and it names, claims and blames somebody for their condition. When we act like victims,we see what everyone else has done against us instead of looking at what God has done for us. A victim constantly looks at the world as an unfair place where other people always seem to have exclusive advantages that explain why others prosper justifying why they can't. A victim is the most susceptible to bit-terness, envy, and vengeful behavior. We can't be witnesses on this earth if we're paralyzed victims who aren't saying and doing productive things. We can't be a witness when we're paralyzed, victimized and not maximized.

Like Esther in the Bible, I have to remind myself that I'm here as a witness no matter what and the kingdom is at hand so I don't have time to be paralyzed by fear. I've had many invi-tations to pity parties and sadly, I attended a lot of them. Of course, they were never as fun as I'd thought they would be once I got there. I mean who throws a great party in a bathroom, the floor of a closet or a car? I think you all get the point here.

When your marriage fails, a loved one dies, you lose your job, struggle with your health, or even find out you've envied a fake cake for eight years, will you be victimized, paralyzed or maximized? You do have a choice but the choices you make all have consequences that can equate to spiritual life or death. So join me in refusing to be victimized because it will cancel your call in life. When we've succumbed to practices of being victimized and paralyzed, we need to repent and just move on because bigger things are at stake! We each have an inheritance in the purpose and plan of God. I still work hard to remove everything out of my life that is not causing me to walk right and be bold in the Lord. Life has taught me to evaluate each situation that arises and make the decision to avoid being victimized and paralyzed and embrace being maximized! In life, I have the chance to step up, step down or step away. Let's all choose to step up!

Scriptures To Help Us Maximize Our Lives:

The wicked man flees though no one pursues, but the righteous are as bold as a lion (Psalm 28:1).

Have I not commanded you? Be strong and courageous. Do not be frightened, and do not be dismayed, for the Lord you God is with you wherever you go (Joshua 1:9).

Fear not, for I am with you; be not dismayed, for I am your God; I will strengthen you, I will help you, I will uphold you with my righteous right hand (Isaiah 41:10).

Yet I still belong to you; you hold my right hand. You guide me with your counsel, leading me to a glorious destiny (Psalm 73:23-24).

"Search me, O God, and know my heart; test me and know my anxious thoughts. Point out anything in me that offends you, and lead me along the path of everlasting life."

Memory Verse - NKJV Isaiah 26:3

"You will keep him in perfect peace, whose mind is stayed on You, because he trusts in You."

Dr. Chapter 8 Teaching Highlights

1. Families that appear to "have it all" are just as vulnerable, if not more likely, to be the target of the enemy's attacks. We need others to shine and be examples just as much as they need the support and prayers of fellow believers.

2. We need to give our hearts a daily check-up, watching for idols that rear up like weeds and pull them out by the roots.

3. A victim mentality comes in quickly and it names, claims and blames somebody for their condition. When we act like victims, we see what everyone else has done against us instead of looking at what God has done for us.

4. A victim is the most susceptible to bitterness, envy, and vengeful behavior. To be spiritually paralyzed is to have the right equipment but be unable use it. We can't be a witness when we're paralyzed, victimized, and not maximized.

1. The Bible tells us to "put on the full armor of God, so that when the day of evil comes, you may be able to stand your ground" (Ephesians 6:13). Using the truth in the scripture regarding the armor, contemplate how different you would behave in difficult situations and instead of being victimized and paralyzed, you would be maximized.

2. James 3:4 tells us that, "The tongue is a small part of the body, but it makes great boasts." Can you think of all the ways your words have indicated fear, worry, misery, complaining, whining, nagging, discouragement, and or negativity?

3. Isaiah 41:10 tells us, "Fear not, for I am with you; be not dismayed, for I am your God; I will strengthen you, I will help you, I will uphold you with my righteous right hand." Conduct a prayer of confession and repentance either as an individual or as a group. Ask God to renew your mind, helping you to speak words of positivity, healing and blessing over your life and the lives of those around you.

4. Is there someone in your life that you need to forgive? Do you need to be forgiven? This is a pivotal point in your journey with God. Right here, right now stop making excuses, stop playing the blame game on circumstances or on people who wronged you. In your personal quiet time, write down every name, every circumstance that you need to be free from by forgiving and moving forward. Share only you are comfortable with as a small group.

5. Using this scripture talk about how you will now begin moving on with your life in a positive manner. "Have I not commanded you? Be strong and courageous. Do not be frightened, and do not be dismayed, for the Lord you God is with you wherever you go" (Joshua 1:9).

Notes

It is the

question

that

causes

the

greatest

turmoil...

Chapter 9

Seeking God for Our Own Style

"Elegance is the only beauty that never fades."
—Audrey Hepburn

I have an embarrassing story that is one of many in my life, but this one ties into seeking God for our own style. Several years ago, I had sudden and serious health issues. Without getting into a long description of all the existing complications 30 percent of us who do survive suffer with, I'll give you the short version. I had a brain hemorrhage further complicated by meningitis just a few days after giving birth to my last child. I survived. Nevertheless, I live with an existing aneurysm. Because of these issues, I have to do a series of annual exams. I don't like these exams because it's a painful reminder of the past. It also confines me into an MRI machine that makes me feel like I'm suffocating. The doctors know plenty of people like me and prescribe a sedative to calm us. It was time for my annual exam, I took the sedative, completed my exams, and my husband brought me back home to rest. He then ran errands and picked up the children from daycare and school.

I was hungry and I stumbled downstairs for the sandwich my husband made for me earlier. I was eating propped by the kitchen counter when the family walked in. All of them even my baby girl who I almost died giving birth to, began laughing. Apparently, I'd taken off my jeans and left everything else on including my new butt-padded underwear. I was so embarrassed I attempted to run back upstairs but forgot I was still under the influence of the sedative and stumbled backward into the kitchen. This all made my family laugh even harder. Finally, I caught a glimpse of myself in a hallway mirror and I couldn't help but join the laughter. I looked like a wrestler, which was very different from the woman in well filled out jeans that left for the MRI that morning. It was just that I wanted to compensate for what I lacked in my nether regions. I wanted to do what I could do to be a masterpiece on the outside. Without the covering of my clothes, everyone including me could see that my new well-shaped bottom was fraudulent. Isn't life like this so often? We try hard to be one thing on the outside to compensate for what we lack inwardly. We'll go through great pains to copy or pursue achieving some else's body, life or destiny. Then one day we get busted, somehow some way it's discovered that we really aren't who we pretended to be and we feel so, well bogus.

Do you want your destiny to be a masterpiece shaped and molded by fraudulence or by God? I know I want the real thing from God but I've had some issues getting there. According to Dr. Tony Evans in his book "Destiny", many people miss their destiny because they try to copy or pursue someone else's destiny. They literally miss the value of their own lives and trade it for an imitation of another's. (Evans 2013). For each of us aspiring to grasp the concept of seeking God for our own style to achieve our destiny we must allow God to use the material he gave us. This material comes in the form of our unique gifts, personalities, and experiences. However, the scripture in (Ephesians 6:14-17) gives us the pattern from which every person must create their own garment:

"Stand firm then, with the belt of truth buckled around your waist, with the breastplate of righteousness in place, and with your feet fitted with the readiness that comes from the gospel of peace. In addition to all this, take up the shield of faith, with which you can extinguish all the flaming arrows of the evil one. Take the helmet of salvation and the sword of the

Spirit, which is the word of God" (Ephesians 6:14-17).

There is a most important question in this world. From the very beginning of time, I promise you this has captivated the hearts of many throughout their lives. Its the question that we use to torture others and ourselves. The question that causes the greatest turmoil on Monday mornings and is to blame for causing many of us to run late that we must ask every single day. What should I wear? While we have churches, debating whether to come as you are or dress in your Sunday best God is most concerned about our spiritual dress. In Matthew 22 the parable of the wedding feast describes God's examination of our garments and the consequences of coming up short:

"But when the king came in to see the guests, he noticed a man there who was not wearing wedding clothes.12 He asked, 'How did you get in here without wedding clothes, friend?' The man was speechless.

"Then the king told the attendants, 'Tie him hand and foot, and throw him outside, into the darkness, where there will be weeping and gnashing of teeth.'

"For many are invited, but few are chosen (Matthew 22:11-14).

According to writer and pastor, Charles Spurgeon:

"....The wedding garment represents anything which is indispensable to a Christian, but which the unrenewed heart is not willing to accept, anything which the Lord ordains to be a necessary attendant of salvation, against which selfishness rebels.... The wedding dress is a holy character, the imparted righteousness which the Holy Spirit works in us and which is equally necessary as a proof of grace..." (Spurgeon).

There was a time in my life when I was 21 and I was an under-dresser. Sure, my clothes were skimpy too. I had Madonna and Boy George as role models so I wavered between wearing tight dresses with leg warmers or cut offs and lumber jack shirts. Spiritually my outfit could fit in the back pocket of my acid-washed jeans. If people found out I ever attended church they'd be shocked because I spent so much time in the clubs it wouldn't seem possible I had time for God. I gave Him the leftovers.

As long as the weather was good or I didn't have something better to do, I'd show up to church. Occasionally, I'd go a little beyond and get involved in something over the edge like a Bible study but the time constraints would often get in my way. Dressing appropriately became my focus, since I was trying to figure out my life after college. I began to ask my parents of all people about my appearance the night before interviews. One day they surprised me with several new suits and days later, I got a job teaching! My days of under-dressing were over!

Yet, on the weekend, I really let go of myself. I became a sloppy dresser and lazed around in sweats and workout clothes until Monday. My spiritual dress was similar. I didn't take my Christian walk seriously and no one viewed me as any type of role model for Christianity. I didn't pay a lot of attention to how I behaved outside of church. I was a free-flowing Christian and my walk rarely had an impact on anyone. Church attendance was optional because I was dating and hanging out with my friends and that often conflicted with my plans. When it was time to go to work, I still asked my parents what I should wear.

Finally, the day came when all that dating seemed to pay off I'd thought I met Mr. Right we got married and had a kid right away. I felt like more of an adult at 26 now that I had a child to rear. I decided to dress more on the casual side on the weekends so I'd seem more grown up. I also thought I needed to bring my little girl to church. I became a casual dresser outwardly and spiritually. People at work had an idea that I was a Christian but I'm sure they thought of me as the light version. I began to get more involved in church ministry and make friends in the church but the relationships never seemed to go beyond the surface. On Monday mornings, I now asked my husband advice on - what I should wear.

My fairytale didn't last very long. With the ink barely dry from the marriage certificate next thing, I knew I was looking at new ink on divorce papers. Yet, I was doing great at work and I began to throw myself into church ministry. Before long, I was shining in and outside of church as an over-dressed woman. I began to over exert myself in extra work projects and stretch myself to the limit. I was working long hours but I had a great paycheck and seemed very spiritual to my friends and coworkers. My outward life screamed, "Super-Saint" but within I was suffering. I was preoccupied with my image and had the sinking feeling that nothing I did was enough to fill the void in my life. Weekday mornings even without parents and a husband around, I asked my two-year-old advice of what I should wear.

By the time, I reached 35 I'd been married and divorced again with another child to raise. I now was the most over-dressed person at work as I was the principal. I was a little more disillusioned about church so I kept more of a distance. Outwardly, I seemed very spiritual and still led several church ministries. People began to seek me out for advice and look to me as a church leader. My outward spirit was over-dressed for the ministries I served. I seemed sanctified in church. Yet, I needed authenticity in relationships to help me face what I was going through. I found that church folks were gossipy, judgmental, and downright mean sometimes. Then when Mondays came along, I had two girls to ask - what should I wear?

Finally, I got to a desperate point. I was frustrated, surrounded by people but feeling deserted. With my face pressed against the bathroom mirror, I asked myself that most important question. "Katherine what should you wear?" Right then, I realized my problem. When it came to directing the most important question, I looked to myself and everyone else but God for the answer. I sat on the sink's cold edge and prayed for God to help me put on what was lacking. Anyone else would've thought I was crazy crying over what to wear. It didn't matter, God knew I needed much more than physical clothes, but armor custom designed, an original little black dress made exclusively for me.

On a weekday morning, two years later before I got dressed, I was feeling self-conscious and growing out of every maternity outfit I had. Of course, I asked my new husband- advice on what I should wear. This time though I'd got up and asked God the same question but regarding my spiritual dress. In the words of Charles Spurgeon who breaks down the meaning of Matthew 22:11-14, "Everything will have to be tested by a heart-searching God, and if, when he comes to search us, we are found wanting, we shall be expelled even from the marriage feast itself; for there is a way to hell from the very gates of heaven" (Spurgeon).

I felt blessed knowing that I had Jesus to clothe me and armor me as never before. We are protected when we put Christ on. We don't need a cheap imitation of his glory. He is our truth and provides our integrity. He protects our hearts and is the peace of our lives as we stand firm in him. He is our shield of faith, our hope, in Christ; we have victory in our minds. When we put on the armor, we are literally putting on Christ because the armor is a figurative explanation of Christ himself. When pressed to ask that most important question regarding our spiritual dress, "What should I wear today?" It is best to call on the Lord himself. The scripture confirms, "It is because of him that you are in Christ Jesus, who has become for us wisdom from God—that is, our righteousness, holiness and redemption" (1st Corinthians 1:30).

"Stand firm then, with the belt of truth buckled around your waist, with the breastplate of righteousness in place, and with your feet fitted with the readiness that comes from the gospel of peace. In addition to all this, take up the shield of faith, with which you can extinguish all the flaming arrows of the evil one. Take the helmet of salvation and the sword of the Spirit, which is the word of God."

Memory Verse – 1 Corinthians 1:30

"It is because of him that you are in *Christ Jesus,* *who has become for us* wisdom *from God —that is,* our *righteousness, holiness and redemption."*

Dr. Chapter 9 Teaching Highlights

1. For each of us aspiring to grasp the concept of seeking God for our own style to achieve our destiny we must allow God to use the unique gifts, personalities, and experiences he has given us.

2. We are protected when we put Christ on.

3. When we put on the armor, we are literally putting on Christ because the armor is a figurative explanation of Christ himself. When pressed to ask that most important question regarding our spiritual dress, "What should I wear today?" It is best to call on the Lord himself.

Read Matthew 22:11-14, "But when the king came in to see the guests, he noticed a man there who was not wearing wedding clothes. He asked, 'How did you get in here without wedding clothes, friend?' The man was speechless.

"Then the king told the attendants, 'Tie him hand and foot, and throw him outside, into the darkness, where there will be weeping and gnashing of teeth.

"For many are invited, but few are chosen."

The words of Charles Spurgeon breaks down the meaning of Matthew 22:11-14 by explaining, "Everything will have to be tested by a heart-searching God, and if, when he comes to search us, we are found wanting, we shall be expelled even from the marriage feast itself; for there is a way to hell from the very gates of heaven" (Spurgeon).

This interpretation from a respected theologian is shocking and is a reminder that we need to constantly search our own hearts so that we are never found wanting. I believe the worst issue for someone being expelled from the wedding feast is the oblivion experienced in seeing how lacking his or her heart had become.

1. Have you ever shown up to an event or place where either you or others were dressed inappropriately?

2. Do you believe you are one of the few who will be chosen, why? Are there any people that concern you regarding their salvation? If so, pray over them. Think about how, when and where you will share the gospel with them.

3. Reread Ephesians 6:14-17. Right now, what part of your spiritual armor needs the most attention?

Notes

We each
have an
inheritance
in the
purpose
and plan
of God.

Chapter 10

Discarding the Old Garments

"Anyone can get dressed up and glamorous,
but it is how people dress in their days off
that are the most intriguing."
—Alexander Wang

Have you ever held onto someone or something longer than you should? Maybe it's an unhealthy connection to a former boyfriend when you're in a committed relationship or married. Perhaps it's a pile of outdated magazines or stacks of old files and papers. It could be clothes you haven't worn in years but for some reason you hold onto them. Do you have a closet, room, drawer or garage packed with stuff you'll never use but you can't seem to part with? Did you know that this strange, yet common, behavior indicates a state of discontentment in some area of our lives (Structure with Sarah 2011). Did you also know that discontentment is a result of unresolved emotions? You may wonder what a closet packed with unworn clothing and a few numbers connecting us to our not so distant past may have to do with our relationship with God. In all things, the Lord asks us to "consider our ways or give careful thought to our ways" (Haggai 1:5).

Then the word of the Lord came through the prophet Haggai: "Is it a time for you yourselves to be living in your paneled houses, while this house remains a ruin?" Now this is what the Lord Almighty says: "Give careful thought to your ways. You have planted much, but harvested little. You eat, but never have enough. You drink, but never have your fill. You put on clothes, but are not warm. You earn wages, only to put them in a purse with holes in it." This is what the Lord Almighty says: "Give careful thought to your ways. Go up into the mountains and bring down timber and build my house, so that I may take pleasure in it and be honored," says the Lord. "You expected much, but see, it turned out to be little. What you brought home, I blew away. Why?" declares the Lord Almighty. "Because of my house, which remains a ruin, while each of you is busy with your own house. Therefore, because of you the heavens have withheld their dew and the earth its crops. I called for a drought on the fields and the mountains, on the grain, the new wine, the olive oil and everything else the ground produces, on people and livestock, and on all the labor of your hands" (Haggai 1:3- 10).

In the book of Haggai, the minor prophet reminded the people of the Lord's message that they were to "consider their ways" and that they'd neglected rebuilding the temple. He reveals to them that since they chose preoccupation with their own lives and obviously stopped putting God first, everything they sow would result in a small harvest. Ironically, the Bible says in a number of places that the people already had the wood provided by the king of Persia 15 years prior. He specifically gave them the wood to re-build the temple when they left Babylon. This scripture illustrates that if you return to the Lord he can sustain you through the rough times. This is a great reminder to us even now that we should trust in God and believe in Him despite what is happening in the world around us. To illustrate this point, I think of the many times I've organized my closet only to turn around in a few months and find it in a disheveled state once again. It's frustrating when this happens because it's hard to find things and to know exactly what I have.

After several moves and many attempts at cleaning my own closet, I knew it was time to part ways with clothing that associated me with my former profession as a school principal. I knew I wouldn't do a proper job myself so I hired help. I got the assistance of an organizer used to headstrong hoarders of memories, materialism and meaning (Structure with Sarah 2011). In the same manner, we need the help of the Holy Spirit to spiritually discern what to let go of and what to keep in our hearts. There are idols that accumulate. Some idols are more obvious than others are. While there are some that are obscure and difficult to detect. Over the years, I've developed a way to attack spiritual cleaning using the following tactics:

1. Practice to take off the past.

2. Use life's dilemmas to move to new levels.

3. Shed the clutter.

4. Find new ways to organize time, thoughts & emotions.

5. Simplify life!

These tactics also have a tangible use in taking practical steps to avoid materialism. I found that when I address the idols that accumulate in my life, like a cluttered closet, I'm able to make real progress in the area of my finances by doing the following:

1. Give tithes and offerings to God first before all else.

2. Create and follow a budget, save money.

3. Give things away.

4. Pray about purchases.

5. Avoid the trap of debt.

6. Volunteer.

7. Avoid isolation and secrets.

8. Avoid friendships with pressure and manipulation.

9. Work on being a good friend.

Notes

"This is what the Lord Almighty says: 'Give careful thought to your ways. Go up into the mountains and bring down timber and build my house, so that I may take pleasure in it and be honored, says the Lord. You expected much, but see, it turned out to be little. What you brought home, I blew away. Why? declares the Lord Almighty. Because of my house, which remains a ruin, while each of you is busy with your own house. Therefore, because of you the heavens have withheld their dew and the earth its crops. I called for a drought on the fields and the mountains, on the grain, the new wine, the olive oil and everything else the ground produces, on people and livestock, and on all the labor of your hands."

Memory Verse - Haggai 1:5

" *This is what the Lord Almighty says:* Give careful thought to your ways. "

Dr. Chapter 10 Teaching Highlights

1. Preoccupation with our own lives results in a small harvest.

2. If you return to the Lord he can sustain you through the rough times.

3. We need the help of the Holy Spirit to spiritually discern what to let go and what to keep in our hearts.

4. Practice taking off the past.

6. Take practical steps to avoid materialism.

1. Anything we place on a pedestal above all else has the ability to compete with our walk with God. This can even be a good thing, like loving our careers, family, exercise routines or bank accounts but if it becomes an idol, it has to be rooted out or put back into a proper place. Evaluate if there is anything in your life that is currently competing with God. If so how can you actively change this today? If not, what are those things that could have the potential to compromise your walk with God?

2. Sometimes we may not hold onto clothing or things that need cleaning but we may be holding onto behaviors that need changing. Are you easily manipulated? Do you give up your power easily in decision-making? Do you constantly try to keep the peace by never saying how you feel about something?

3. Bringing glory to God should always be the end product of all our problems. The Bible tells us, "My suffering was good for me, for it taught me to pay attention to your decrees" (NLT Psalm 119:71). Sometimes life throws us a curve ball with an especially disturbing news report, the impact of terrorism on our country, the economy, etc. How will you purposely use life's dilemmas to move to new levels?

4. How will you shed the clutter of unhealthy thoughts, emotions and people?

5. How will you find new ways to organize time, thoughts and emotions when a void has been created by shedding excess?

6. How will you make life simpler?

7. Are there triggers in your life that cause you to repeat bad behavior?

8. What active steps are you taking to nurture your gifts? Are you using them to glorify God and others? How?

Notes

I've
noticed a
disturbing
trend where
the church
and secular
establish-
ments have
traded
places.

Chapter 11

Nakedness and Healing

"I wanted to give a woman
comfortable clothes that would flow with her body.
A woman is closest to being naked when she is well-dressed."
— Coco Chanel

Have you ever struggled to put together a puzzle only to find that the reason you struggled so much was that you were missing a piece? Once you found that missing piece the entire picture came together. I often see the same correlation when I'm trying to put together an outfit. Sometimes I'll have beautiful pieces of clothing to wear but it just doesn't flow together. Often it just takes adding the scarf, jewelry or switching an article of clothing to create an outfit that flows and is so comfortable it's as if your look is as effortless as being naked. What's important is you aren't actually naked!

I'm sure by now we all realize that Adam and Eve struggled with similar wardrobe malfunctions. They too knew what it was to struggle to put together an outfit and come up short. They were the first sinners to have to stand before God to be called into account and explain their choices. Prior to their disobedience, they never worried about their nakedness. After sin entered the world through their actions, they sensed the guilt, shame, and humiliation that come from disobedience and hence spiritual nakedness. Now, the former physical and spiritual nakedness they experienced symbolized innocence, vulnerability and child-like faith was gone. Intuitively they sensed their nakedness had to be covered up and in a sense, they were correct. Unfortunately, their attempt at covering their nakedness was inadequate as they rushed to throw together an outfit with whatever was easily available at the time — some fig leaves. God replaced their inferior covering with a much more acceptable garment.

The point of this chapter hinges on this very lesson: God has a standard for covering the type of spiritual nakedness that brings guilt, shame and humiliation. His standard is by means of death. This makes any covering we come up with, worthless. This lesson teaches us some fundamental concepts about coming into the presence of God that we need, both literally and spiritually. It addresses the attitude of "come as you are" a mantra many churches have adopted. The notion of acceptance of those seeking a relationship with Christ, but may not understand how to dress to attend church is understandable. Unfortunately, if this attitude is applied wrongfully it can numb us as practicing believers. We can begin behaving in a way that tells God church is just another place and what we wear to worship him doesn't matter.

I've noticed a disturbing trend where the church and secular establishments have traded places. Recently, I was at a hair salon where there were close to 50 different ads and fliers on the counter and bulletin board most of which advertised nightclubs, plays and comedy shows in the area. None of these fliers advertised Christian establishments. However, a clear theme resonated on almost every piece of literature. There were instructions on the appropriate attire in order to gain entry. Some places even had a message from the management explaining what type of clothing would or would not be acceptable. Before arriving, anyone who wanted to attend any of these establishments and read the requirements in advance would have a clear expectation of what was required to guarantee their entrance.

If we all truly understood the depth of what it took on the cross for us to be able to put on Christ, we might spend more time asking ourselves, as we dressed for worship, if our outfit is truly a matter of respect or disrespect. For the believer, this often boils down to a misunderstanding of what God requires and that is a reverence for the prime covering—Christ's sacrifice. God dressed Adam and Eve in the finest of clothing that involved tremendous sacrifice. God calls us to do the same both physically and spiritually. God clearly wants us to conform to Him and the pattern he created. In the Bible there are practical applications we can learn from, such as seem in (Revelation 3:17) "You say, 'I am rich; I have acquired wealth and do not need a thing.' But you do not realize that you are wretched, pitiful, poor, blind and naked." We don't come into God's presence with the mindset that He needs to conform to us.

"For the wages of sin is death, but the gift of God is eternal life in Christ Jesus our Lord" (Romans 6:23). The term "wages" may be unfamiliar but some comparative terms are; earning, pay or salary. Hence, the verse compares our sin to working to earning death. Then, the next half of the verse brings us hope by explaining that God has a way out of this problem by substituting our death wage with eternal life in Christ. It sounds like such a simple trade off, even an unfair one in our favor. The principle that the Bible teaches here is that we are always to give our best to God. The death penalty is imposed when we fail. This, then, teaches another lesson. Although, the curse is blamed on Adam and Eve, really the entire human race sinned in Adam and Eve. All they did was clearly represent all of humanity at the beginning of time on Earth. Since the wages of sin is death, and all have sinned, all of us have to receive that wage. Fortunately, God prearranged for another to receive those wages. The perfect lamb, Jesus Christ the son of God on who never sinned, became the substitute for us.

The other aspect of this teaching also involves another death, which is ours. However, it is not a physical death but a spiritual one. The Bible tells us,

"What shall we say then? Shall we continue in sin that grace may abound? Certainly not! How shall we who died to sin live any longer in it?...Knowing this, that our old man was crucified with Him, that the body of sin might be done away with, that we should no longer be slaves of sin. For he who has died has been freed from sin. Now if we died with Christ, we believe that we shall also live with Him" (KJV Romans 6:1-2, 6-8).

This aspect of dying isn't literal. It is dying to self and accepting that this is achieved through repentance. Once we understand that we are sinners, we need God's forgiveness because we're guilty of breaking His law and we've earned death, and then we truly put on Christ.

"You say, 'I am rich; I have acquired wealth and do not need a thing.' But you do not realize that you are wretched, pitiful, poor, blind, and naked."

Memory Verse – Romans 6:23

"*For the wages of sin is death,*
but the gift of God is eternal life in
Christ Jesus our Lord."

Dr. ❦ Chapter 11 Teaching Highlights

1. God has a standard for covering the type of spiritual nakedness that brings guilt, shame, and humiliation.

2. Some dress as if what we wear to worship God doesn't matter.

3. God dressed Adam and Eve in the finest of clothing that involved tremendous sacrifice. God calls us to do the same both physically and spiritually.

4. Since the wages of sin is death, and all have sinned, all of us have to receive that wage. Fortunately, God prearranged for another to receive those wages. The perfect lamb, Jesus Christ the son of God on who never sinned, became the substitute for us.

1. Can you think of a cause or a person you would willingly lay down your life for? Why?

2. God clearly wants us to conform to Him and the pattern he created. In the Bible there are practical applications we can learn from such as seen in Revelation 3:17, "You say, 'I am rich; I have acquired wealth and do not need a thing.' But you do not realize that you are wretched, pitiful, poor, blind, and naked." We don't come into God's presence with the mindset that He needs to conform to us. Why is it sinful to believe we don't need God?

3. God has a standard for covering the type of spiritual naked-ness that brings guilt, shame, and humiliation. His standard is by means of death. This makes any covering we come up with, worthless. The idea of having a standard of death seems morbid from a loving God. However, God created a way for us to be rescued from a sinful state. This method had to be death so we could rise again with Him in perfection through Christ. In what ways could you be in danger of being spiritually naked (think about the things in your life that have brought shame, guilt and humiliation)?

4. What are some ways you've acted to make yourself feel better but they were only temporary fixes? Why do you this the fix you came up with didn't last?

5. Describe the benefit of each trait in your relationship with God.
   a. Innocence
   b. Vulnerability
   c. Child-like faith

Notes

The world
is slick at
asking the
right
questions
with the
wrong
motives and
solutions.

Chapter 12

Wearing Our Dress Well

"The beauty of a woman is not in the clothes she wears, the figure that she carries, or the way she combs her hair. The beauty of a woman is seen in her eyes, because that is the doorway to her heart, the place where love resides. True beauty in a woman is reflected in her soul. It's the caring that she lovingly gives, the passion that she showsand the beauty of a woman only grows with passing years."
— Audrey Hepburn

By now, we know we have everything it takes to be a feminine warrior capable of battling the challenges separating us from a deeper relationship with God. Yes, we know that we will have ongoing battles, but, despite that, with our armor and lipstick on, we can have an abundant life by cultivating a stronger walk with God, working toward creating healthy family environments and renewing a sense of deeper self-fulfillment in achieving our dreams. Disclaimer: I do need to warn you that even being spiritually armored and accessorized to clean up the messiest spiritual dresser we're going to have to fight a few battles because of a well-known enemy that comes to attack in disguise. Alert: do not get in the ring, keep your armor on, and do what you can, but allow God to do what you can't.

I know this may seem odd after comparing our spiritual armor to a little black dress, but I want you to envision a very badly dressed villain who clearly doesn't like us girls. This villain seems to kick us when we're down, pit our family members and friends against us when we need them the most; cloud our best dreams, and replace them with doubt, frustration and envy; and worst he's wearing our tights! Okay, I think you get the picture, but bear with me, I'm wrapping this thing up and I'm going somewhere with this.

An avid comic-book fan, I've seen just about every Batman movie there is so I was shocked to learn of Heath Ledger's premature death at age 27. The tragedy took place right before the movie he played the infamous villain, the Joker, hit the theaters. After reading Rolling Stone's obituary of Ledger, I'm of the opinion the Joker is one of the culprits to be blamed for Ledger's death. This of course confirms that there is power in the roles we play whether real or make-believe. After all, it's what we believe that becomes our reality. The following lines in the Rolling Stone piece seem to reinforce the idea that the Joker killed Ledger:

"He couldn't seem to disengage; the inexactness bothered him. Ledger had no formal training, and there's this to be said for acting school: it teaches you to approach a role as foreign, as a language you'll temporarily speak. Ledger didn't appear to have that. He needed to dig for (and inhabit) the part of himself that was the character. 'Performance comes from absolutely believing what you're doing,' he said. 'You convince yourself, and believe in the story with all your heart.' It didn't always shut off when a production did, and I think it ground him."

"As The Joker in next summer's The Dark Knight, he will appear as a man severed from all connection. A 'psychopathic, mass-murdering clown with zero empathy,' is how he described it to the New York Times. On set, Michael Caine said the performance sometimes turned so frightening he forgot his own lines" (Rolling Stone Magazine 2008).

If that were not bad enough, on July 20, 2012 James Holmes dressed as the Joker from the movie "The Dark Knight," and to the horror of Colorado movie-goers opened fire on masses of innocent people. The entire time he was mimicking the psychopathic, mass-murdering clown portrayed in the film with zero empathy for anyone. He injured and even paralyzed several of the people he attacked. He killed twelve people in cold blood including a six-year-old girl and her unborn sibling while confining their mother to a wheelchair as a quadriplegic. Why would I share this shocking and grim tale with you today? Well, it's because it's crucial for us to stop and pause to realize that the unthinkable is happening all around us and to us. I also believe we need to be reminded that the unthinkable — who is our enemy, is in disguise, is purposeful, calculated and evil.

By now, you may be saying to yourself, "I don't need to hear any added chaos to the existing things that make me sad such as marital issues, my children, health concerns, finances, terrorism, aging, not being able to ever find the match to socks when I do the laundry and the list goes on!"You may be saying, "I didn't come to this place to feel worse that I already do, I need something to make me feel better!" Well, I have good news for you. There is an unseen benefit to our sadness; the world's escalating madness and the devil's badness! We still win because we're on the winning team. While it may not seem like it from where we are, things are shaping up just as perfectly as the Bible told us it would. Jesus himself explained this in detail in Matthew 24:6-14:

"You will hear of wars and rumors of wars, but see to it that you are not alarmed. Such things must happen, but the end is still to come. Nation will rise against nation, and kingdom against kingdom. There will be famines and earthquakes in various places. All these are the beginning of birth pains. Then you will be handed over to be persecuted and put to death, and you will be hated by all nations because of me. At that time many will turn away from the faith and will betray and hate each other, and many false prophets will

appear and deceive many people. Because of the increase of wickedness, the love of most will grow cold,but the one who stands firm to the end will be saved. And this gospel of the kingdom will be preached in the whole world as a testimony to all nations, and then the end will come."

I'd like to use the infamous question of Batman's Joker and ask,"Why so serious?" Why would I dare to ask you the question why are you so serious, or, to put it another way — why are you so sad? I'm asking you because Satan has constructed this question for each of you in a unique way and it's important for you to be aware when he slides up to you and asks you about your particular state of being. If you're aware, then you'll prepare. You see the world is slick at asking the right questions with the wrong motives and solutions.

A drug dealer, whether dressed in a T-shirt and on a street corner or in a white-coat sitting in a Dr.'s office, asks you about your state and offers you a solution with mind-numbing yet, devastating consequences. A supposed friend asks you about your state then offers you their brand of outlet in sexual promiscuity. A bartender asks you about your state because the more they get customers talking, the more they drink and sales increase. Even your television and movies asks you about your emotional state and offers up the crudest, vile and shocking footage in the form of comedies, dramas, action-thrillers, and horror to provide escapes from your pain. After the curtain closes, you're exposed to more depravity, more very bad ideas and the pain is still there.

God asked our ancestor Adam the question, where are you? God also asked Adam's son, Cain, why he was so sad. God is omnipotent — meaning he knows all but doesn't experience all because He can't sin. Therefore, in posing questions about our whereabouts or our emotional state, what God really wants from us is honesty through self-evaluation based on His truths, confession and a change of heart and behavior. Effectively, Adam would have been correct if he'd answered God by admitting he was lost, got Eve lost and was sorry for messing up. By the way, he needed directions to get back to where his relationship with God began. Cain would've been correct if he'd confessed to being sad because he was jealous of his brother and was too prideful to get some advice on how to provide a better offering. Later, God asked Cain where his brother Able was. Cain would've avoided this confrontation of the murderer he was by taking God's advice from the start and modeling Abel's desirable behavior. This is a disturbing and truthful depiction of human nature. It reveals our tendency to avoid seeing our own sin, doing things our way, and finally killing the very hope that will guide us to a better relationship with God.

Could it be we're drunk on the overflowing fountain of pop-culture? Have we had too many sips from the world's music, movies, comic books, news, tweets, and Facebook posts? Is it that self-pity, gossip, and long, leisurely vacations in the past could be anesthetizing us to the weapons aimed at our faith, our joy and our sense of fun?

You see, the sooner we all realize that there is a real Joker in the world trying to keep us from true joy the better off we are. The Joker is the enemy, Satan who disguises sin as fun, a way out, escapism, self-enlightenment and the like. The reality is the Joker is a false angel of light who pretends to offer us solutions to life's dilemmas and pain when all the while he wants to destroy us. Don't be afraid because while he has tremendous power he isn't all-knowing and his time has an expiration date. Therefore, he cannot compete with the most powerful one and true living God. Jesus said in his word:

"I am the door; if anyone enters through Me, he will be saved, and will go in and out and find pasture. "The thief comes only to steal and kill and destroy; I came that they may have life, and have it abundantly. "I am the good shepherd; the good shepherd lays down His life for the sheep" (John 10: 9-11).

Are you willing to enter into the door that will grant you an abundant life packed with joy to overflowing? Then hear this-

The Action Plan

Empathize with all those who suffer, intervene, and pray for yourself and others who suffer at the hands of the Joker.

Be prepared, be on guard, do not get distracted by the masked villains of the day.

Resist being held hostage by fear or living in oblivion.

Understand we are in a war but also believe the good news and that is -the battle has been fought and won for us a long time ago!

Keep vigilant and keep your joy despite the circumstances.

All we have to do is put one cute little foot in front of another to put space between us and our past hurts, all we have to do is keep standing on the word of God, all we have to do is keep praying. Well, how do we do this you may be saying to yourselves after all this heavy talk?

Key Points of Implementation

Keep your sense of humor or get one, it is terrific armor! One bout of belly laughing can keep an army of demons at bay! Am I the only person or have you too had some of your best laughs at the heart of a crisis? How about while attending a funeral? Do you really think that was an accident? No! It was from God.

Create an army around you for the battle is all around us! Godly family, friends, and prayer partners will successfully combat an attack. Small groups where there is transparency and accountability will keep any enemy in check. Spend time in prayer and reading your Bible as the powerful word of God will rebuke demonic attacks, cure diseases, raise the dead in Christ, and invoke incredible joy in even the most incredible crisis!

Key Scriptures to remember: (Romans 8:18-39)

"I consider that our present sufferings are not worth comparing with the glory that will be revealed in us. For the creation waits in eager expectation for the children of God to be revealed. For the creation was subjected to frustration, not by its own choice, but by the will of the one who subjected it, in hope that the creation itself will be liberated from its bondage to decay and brought into the freedom and glory of the children of God.

"We know that the whole creation has been groaning as in the pains of childbirth right up to the present time. Not only so, but we ourselves, who have the firstfruits of the Spirit, groan inwardly as we wait eagerly for our adoption to sonship, the redemption of our bodies. For in this hope we were saved. But hope that is seen is no hope at all. Who hopes for what they already have? But if we hope for what we do not yet have, we wait for it patiently.

"In the same way, the Spirit helps us in our weakness. We do not know what we ought to pray for, but the Spirit himself intercedes for us through wordless groans. And he who searches our hearts knows the mind of the Spirit, because the Spirit intercedes for God's people in accordance with the will of God.

"And we know that in all things God works for the good of those who love him, whohave been called according to his purpose.For those God foreknew he also predestined to be conformed to the image of his Son, that he might be the firstborn among many brothers and sisters.30 And those he predestined, he also called; those he called, he also justified; those he justified, he also glorified.

"What, then, shall we say in response to these things? If God is for us, who can be against us? He who did not spare his own Son, but gave him up for us all—how will he not also, along with him, graciously give us all things? Who will bring any charge against those whom God has chosen? It is God who justifies. Who then is the one who condemns? No one.

Christ Jesus who died—more than that, who was raised to life—is at the right hand of God and is also interceding for us. Who shall separate us from the love of Christ? Shall trouble or hardship or persecution or famine or nakedness or danger or sword? As it is written:

" 'For your sake we face death all day long; we are considered as sheep to be slaughtered.'

"No, in all these things we are more than conquerors through him who loved us. For I am convinced that neither death nor life, neither angels nor demons,neither the present nor the future, nor any powers, neither height nor depth, nor anything else in all creation, will be able to separate us from the love of God that is in Christ Jesus our Lord."

In summary, I'd like to highlight the following:

- God wants us to hope, but He wants us to hope for something bigger than today.

- God desires for us to believe in Him and the place He is preparing for us.

- It is freeing to live thankfully and expectantly rather than with the restrictions of disappointment, so have some fun!

I'll leave you with some thought-provoking quotes from the same comic-book inspired movies of the Batman series:

"Suffering builds character."

"It's not who I am underneath, but what I do that defines me."

"The night is darkest just before the dawn."

"I am the door; if anyone enters through Me, he will be saved, and will go in and out and find pasture. The thief comes only to steal and kill and destroy; I came that they may have life, and have it abundantly. I am the good shepherd; the good shepherd lays down His life for the sheep."

Memory Verse – Romans 8:18

"I consider that our present sufferings

are not worth comparing

with the glory that will be revealed in us."

Dr. Chapter 12 Teaching Highlights

1. What God really wants from us is honesty through self-evaluation based on His truths, confession and a change of heart and behavior.

2. Like Cain, our tendency to avoid seeing our own sin, doing things our way, and finally killing the very hope that will guide us to a better relationship with God.

3. God wants us to hope, but He wants us to hope for something bigger than today.

4. It is freeing to live thankfully and expectantly rather than with the restrictions of disappointment, so have some fun!

1. Could it be we're drunk on the overflowing fountain of pop-culture? Have we had too many sips from the world's music, movies, comic books, news, tweets, and face book posts? Could self-pity, gossip, and long leisurely vacations in the past be anesthetizing us to the weapons aimed at our faith, our joy, and our sense of fun? On a scale of 1-10 with 1 being the lowest and 10 being the highest estimate how you rate the effectiveness of armor of God you wear to protect you?

2. "I am the door; if anyone enters through Me, he will be saved, and will go in and out and find pasture. The thief comes only to steal and kill and destroy; I came that they may have life, and have it abundantly. I am the good shepherd; the good shepherd lays down His life for the sheep" (NKJV John 10: 9-11). Explain why you are willing to enter into the door that will grant you an abundant life packed with joy to overflowing.

3. God desires for us to believe in Him and the place He is preparing for us. What is it you're hoping for that is beyond your ability? (This could be a personal goal, etc.)

4. Pretend you are getting prepared to enter heaven. Prepare an acceptance speech for the reward of salvation you're about to receive. Remember God is in the audience so make it good!

5. Are there things (dreams, people, and goals) in your life you've given up on? Why, or why not?

6. Do you honestly live thankfully and expectantly? In what ways does your life reflect this?

Notes

Essentials for Every Spiritual Wardrobe

(New American Bible Revised Edition)

Put on

the armor

of God so

that you

may be able

to stand

firm against

the tactics

of the devil.

There is no way to be a Christian but walk with faith through life that is comparable to a battlefield. At all times, we should be ready to share and spread the gospel by our good works, willingness to choose good over evil and by our diligent obedience to God. God gives us the tools to prosper in life that takes place primarily within our mind and the spiritual realm. Throughout the Bible, literal imagery depicts how to protect our vital assets and how to use them to benefit others, the kingdom of God, and ourselves.

Ephesians 6:10-20: "Finally, draw your strength from the Lord and from his mighty power. Put on the armor of God so that you may be able to stand firm against the tactics of the devil. For our struggle is not with flesh and blood but with the principalities, with the powers, with the world rulers of this present darkness, with the evil spirits in the heavens. Therefore, put on the armor of God, that you may be able to resist on the evil day and, having done everything, to hold your ground. So stand fast with your loins girded in truth, clothed with righteousness as a breastplate, and your feet shod in readiness for the gospel of peace. In all circumstances, hold faith as a shield, to quench all [the] flaming arrows of the evil one. And take the helmet of salvation and the sword of the Spirit, which is the word of God. With all prayer and supplication, pray at every opportunity in the Spirit. To that end, be watchful with all perseverance and supplication for all the holy ones and also for me, that speech may be given me to open my mouth, to make known with boldness the mystery of the gospel for which I am an ambassador in chains, so that I may have the courage to speak as I must."

Romans 13:11-12: "And do this because you know the time; it is the hour now for you to awake from sleep. For our salvation is nearer now than when we first believed; the night is advanced, the day is at hand. Let us then throw off the works of darkness (and) put on the armor of light..."

The Helmet of Salvation

Our mind is the first thing to come under attack. This is why the Helmet of Salvation is the most necessary defensive weapon to protect our emotions, intellect, and reasoning. Our thoughts become our actions, our actions become our habits, our habits become our character, and our character becomes our destiny. With the right thoughts, salvation is our destiny.

1 Peter 1:13-19: "Therefore, gird up the loins of your mind, live soberly, and set your hopes completely on the grace to be brought to you at the revelation of Jesus Christ. Like obedient children, do not act in compliance with the desires of your former ignorance but, as he who called you is holy, be holy yourselves in every aspect of your conduct, for it is written, "Be holy because I [am] holy. Now if you invoke as Father him who judges impartially according to each one's works, conduct yourselves with reverence during the time of your sojourning, realizing that you were ransomed from your futile conduct, handed on by your ancestors, not with perishable things like silver or gold, but with the precious blood of Christ as of a spotless unblemished lamb."

Romans 12:2: "Do not conform yourselves to this age but be transformed by the renewal of your mind, that you may discern what is the will of God, what is good and pleasing and perfect."

1 Thessalonians 5:8: "But since we are of the day, let us be sober, putting on the breastplate of faith and love and the helmet that is hope for salvation."

Isaiah 59:17: "He put on justice as his breastplate, victory as a helmet on his head; He clothed himself with garments of vengeance, wrapped himself in a mantle of zeal."

Jeremiah 46:3-4: "Prepare buckler and shield! Move forward to battle! Harness the horses, charioteers, mount up! Fall in, with helmets on; polish your spears, put on your armor."

1 Corinthians 2:16: "For "who has known the mind of the Lord, so as to counsel him?" But we have the mind of Christ."

Philippians 2:5: "Have among yourselves the same attitude that is also yours in Christ Jesus, Who, though he was in the form of God, did not regard equality with God something to be grasped."

1 Peter 4:1-2: "Therefore, since Christ suffered in the flesh, arm yourselves also with the same attitude (for whoever suffers in the flesh has broken with sin), so as not to spend what remains of one's life in the flesh on human desires, but on the will of God."

2 Corinthians 10:3-6: "For, although we are in the flesh, we do not battle according to the flesh, for the weapons of our battle are not of flesh but are enormously powerful, capable of destroying fortresses. We destroy arguments and every pretension raising itself against the knowledge of God, and take every thought captive in obedience to Christ, and we are ready to punish every disobedience, once your obedience is complete."

Ephesians 4:10-16: " The one who descended is also the one who ascended far above all the heavens, that he might fill all things. And he gave some as apostles, others as prophets, others as evangelists, others as pastors and teachers, to equip the holy ones for the work of ministry, for building up the body of Christ, until we all attain to the unity of faith and knowledge of the Son of God, to mature manhood, to the extent of the full stature of Christ, so that we may no longer be infants, tossed by waves and swept along by every wind of teaching arising from human trickery, from their cunning in the interests of deceitful scheming. Rather, living the truth in love, we should grow in every way into him who is the head, Christ, from whom the whole body, joined and held together by every supporting ligament, with the proper functioning of each part, brings about the body's growth and builds itself up in love."

The breastplate is a protective piece that literally and symbolically protects our heart and vital organs. The Bible tells us that the spirit is alive because of righteousness (Romans 8:10). This points to the significance of being able to distinguish between good and evil based on God's standards of truths (1st Kings 3:9).

1 Corinthians 1:30-31: "It is due to him that you are in Christ Jesus, who became for us wisdom from God, as well as righteousness, sanctification, and redemption, so that, as it is written, "Whoever boasts, should boast in the Lord."

1 Thessalonians 5:8: "But since we are of the day, let us be sober, putting on the breastplate of faith and love and the helmet that is hope for salvation."

Isaiah 59:17: "He put on justice as his breastplate, victory as a helmet on his head; He clothed himself with garments of vengeance, wrapped himself in a mantle of zeal."

Jeremiah 46:3-4: "Prepare buckler and shield! Move forward to battle! Harness the horses, charioteers, mount up! Fall in, with helmets on; polish your spears, put on your armor."

Romans 8:10: "But if Christ is in you, although the body is dead because of sin, the spirit is alive because of righteousness."

Philippians 3:8-11: "More than that, I even consider everything as a loss because of the supreme good of knowing Christ Jesus my Lord. For his sake I have accepted the loss of all things and I consider them so much rubbish, that I may gain Christ 9 and be found in him, not having any righteousness of my own based on the law but that which comes through faith in Christ, the righteousness from God, depending on faith 10 to know him and the power of his resurrection and [the] sharing of his sufferings by being conformed to his death, if somehow I may attain the resurrection from the dead."

1 John 2:1: "My children, I am writing this to you so that you may not commit sin. But if anyone does sin, we have an Advocate with the Father, Jesus Christ the righteous one."

Exodus 28:15: "The breast-piece of decision you shall also have made, embroidered like the ephod with gold thread and violet, purple, and scarlet yarn on cloth of fine linen twined."

1 Kings 3:9: "Give your servant, therefore, a listening heart to judge your people and to distinguish between good and evil. For who is able to give judgment for this vast people of yours?"

Psalm 94:15: "Judgment shall again be just, and all the upright of heart will follow it."

Proverbs 2:6-8: "6 For the LORD gives wisdom, from his mouth come knowledge and understanding; 7 He has success in store for the upright, is the shield of those who walk honestly, Guarding the paths of justice, protecting the way of his faithful ones..."

1 John 2:1b

...we have an Advocate with the Father,

Jesus Christ the righteous one.

A shield puts distance between a Christian and the enemy. Our faith is a strong fence that defends us from spiritual attacks. The benefit of keeping our faith fortified is it destroys the lies and schemes aimed at destroying us and or our relationship with God.

Romans 10:17: "Thus faith comes from what is heard, and what is heard comes through the word of Christ."

Psalms 35:1-3: "Oppose, O LORD, those who oppose me; war upon those who make war upon me. Take up the shield and buckler; rise up in my defense. Brandish lance and battle-ax against my pursuers. Say to my soul, 'I am your salvation.'"

Psalms 3:4: "But you, LORD, are a shield around me; my glory, you keep my head high."

Psalms 33:20: "Our soul waits for the LORD, he is our help and shield."

Proverbs 30:5-6: "Every word of God is tested, he is a shield to those who take refuge in him. Add nothing to his words, lest he reprimand you, and you be proved a liar."

Hebrews 11, James 2, Romans 4: Several references to "faith."

Romans 10:17

"Thus faith

comes

from what

is heard,

and what is

heard comes

through the

word of

Christ."

*The sword of the spirit is the only offensive weapon
described on the armor of God. The Bible makes reference
the power of the sword as dual for both the user for edifica-
tion and for the battlefield. Its power is in the word of God
(Hebrews 4:12) and in the power of Christ (Revelation 19:15).*

Hebrews 4:12-13:"Indeed, the word of God is living and effec-
tive, sharper than any two-edged sword, penetrating even
between soul and spirit, joints and marrow, and able to discern
reflections and thoughts of the heart. 13 No creature is concealed
from him, but everything is naked and exposed to the eyes of
him to whom we must render an account."

Jeremiah 46:3-4: "Prepare buckler and shield! Move forward to
battle! Harness the horses, charioteers, mount up! Fall in, with
helmets on; polish your spears, put on your armor.

2 Corinthians 6:1-10: "Working together, then, we appeal to
you not to receive the grace of God in vain. For he says: "In an
acceptable time I heard you, and on the day of salvation I helped
you." Behold, now is a very acceptable time; behold, now is the
day of salvation. We cause no one to stumble in anything, in
order that no fault may be found with our ministry; on the con-
trary, in everything we commend ourselves as ministers of God,
through much endurance, in afflictions, hardships, constraints,
beatings, imprisonments, riots, labors, vigils, fasts; by purity,
knowledge, patience, kindness, in a holy spirit, in unfeigned
love, in truthful speech, in the power of God; with weapons
of righteousness at the right and at the left; through glory and
dishonor, insult and praise. We are treated as deceivers and yet
are truthful; as unrecognized and yet acknowledged; as dying
and behold we live; as chastised and yet not put to death; as

sorrowful yet always rejoicing; as poor yet enriching many; as having nothing and yet possessing all things."

Psalms 149:1-10: "Hallelujah! Sing to the LORD a new song, his praise in the assembly of the faithful. Let Israel be glad in its maker, the people of Zion rejoice in their king. Let them praise his name in dance, make music with tambourine and lyre. For the LORD takes delight in his people, honors the poor with victory. Let the faithful rejoice in their glory, cry out for joy on their couches, with the praise of God in their mouths, and a two-edged sword in their hands, to bring retribution on the nations, punishment on the peoples, to bind their kings in shackles, their nobles in chains of iron, to execute the judgments decreed for them— such is the glory of all God's faithful. Hallelujah!"

Revelation 1:16: "In his right hand he held seven stars. A sharp two-edged sword came out of his mouth, and his face shone like the sun at its brightest."

Revelation 2:16: "Therefore, repent. Otherwise, I will come to you quickly and wage war against them with the sword of my mouth.

Revelation 19:15: "Out of his mouth came a sharp sword to strike the nations. He will rule them with an iron rod, and he himself will tread out in the wine press the wine of the fury and wrath of God the almighty."

Ezekiel 21 & 32: Several references to "sword."

The belt on the actual Roman Armor held everything in place. For instance, when Elijah ran in 1st Kings 18:46 he girded his clothes or tucked it into his belt. In other words, the belt was used to get the robe out the way. It kept the breast-plate secure and held the sword in place. Without a belt, a soldier would be defenseless. In reality, it is God's belt we put on as we surround ourselves with God's word (John 17:17). As in Roman times we face the same understanding that to put on the belt is to be properly prepared.

1 Peter 5:8-10: "Be sober and vigilant. Your opponent the devil is prowling around like a roaring lion looking for [someone] to devour. Resist him, steadfast in faith, knowing that your fellow believers throughout the world undergo the same sufferings. The God of all grace who called you to his eternal glory through Christ [Jesus] will himself restore, confirm, strengthen, and establish you after you have suffered a little."

Luke 4:1-13: 1 Filled with the Holy Spirit, Jesus returned from the Jordan and was led by the Spirit into the desert for forty days, to be tempted by the devil. He ate nothing during those days, and when they were over he was hungry. The devil said to him, "If you are the Son of God, command this stone to become bread." Jesus answered him, "It is written, 'One does not live by bread alone.'" Then he took him up and showed him all the kingdoms of the world in a single instant. The devil said to him, "I shall give to you all this power and their glory; for it has been handed over to me, and I may give it to whomever I wish. All this will be yours, if you worship me." Jesus said to him in reply, "It is written: 'You shall worship the Lord, your God, and him alone shall you serve.'" Then he led him to Jerusalem, made him stand on the parapet of the temple, and said to him, "If you are the Son of God, throw yourself down from here, for it is written:

'He will command his angels concerning you, to guard you,' and: 'With their hands they will support you, lest you dash your foot against a stone.'" Jesus said to him in reply, "It also says, 'You shall not put the Lord, your God, to the test.'" When the devil had finished every temptation, he departed from him for a time.

Isaiah 11:5: "Justice shall be the band around his waist, and faithfulness a belt upon his hips."

1 Kings 18:46: "But the hand of the LORD was on Elijah. He girded up his clothing and ran before Ahab as far as the approaches to Jezreel."

Ephesians 4:25-27: "Therefore, putting away falsehood, speak the truth, each one to his neighbor, for we are members one of another. Be angry but do not sin; do not let the sun set on your anger, and do not leave room for the devil."

John 4:24: "God is Spirit, and those who worship him must worship in Spirit and truth."

Colossians 3:8-10: "But now you must put them all away: anger, fury, malice, slander, and obscene language out of your mouths. Stop lying to one another, since you have taken off the old self with its practices and have put on the new self, which is being renewed, for knowledge, in the image of its creator."

2 Thessalonians 8-10:"And then the lawless one will be revealed, whom the Lord [Jesus] will kill with the breath of his mouth and render powerless by the manifestation of his coming, the one whose coming springs from the power of Satan in every mighty deed and in signs and wonders that lie, and in every wicked deceit for those who are perishing because they have not accepted the love of truth so that they may be saved."

The Roman soldier had to have protective shields over their feet to avoid stepping onto something that could injure their feet or worse expose their feet to the weapons of the enemy. Often soldiers wouldn't have the luxury of horses or chariots and the large majority traveled on foot. Therefore, the protection of their feet was paramount. Likewise, a Christian walks the path of life and sets an example to the people they wish to disciple. Their feet are the lives they lead readily available to share the gospel and go where God would have them spread the good news of Christ their Savior.

John 1:1: tells us we have had protection from evil since before we were created: "In the beginning was the Word, and the Word was with God, and the Word was God." We only have to walk in the path of the living Word of Christ Jesus.

Ephesians 2: 17-18: "For he is our peace...He came and preached peace to you who were far off and peace to those who were near, for through him we both have access in one Spirit to the Father. So then you are no longer strangers and sojourners, but you are fellow citizens with the holy ones and members of the household of God, built upon the foundation of the apostles and prophets, with Christ Jesus himself as the capstone."

Proverbs 4:26-27: "Survey the path for your feet, and all your ways will be sure. Turn neither to right nor to left, keep your foot far from evil."

Romans 10:15: "And how can people preach unless they are sent? As it is written, "How beautiful are the feet of those who bring [the] good news!"

1 Corinthians 1:5: "Now I am reminding you, brothers, of the

gospel I preached to you, which you indeed received and in which you also stand. Through it you are also being saved, if you hold fast to the word I preached to you, unless you believed in vain. For I handed on to you as of first importance what I also received: that Christ died for our sins in accordance with the scriptures; that he was buried; that he was raised on the third day in accordance with the scriptures; that he appeared to Cephas, then to the Twelve..."

Isaiah 52:7: "How beautiful upon the mountains are the feet of the one bringing good news, announcing peace, bearing good news, announcing salvation, saying to Zion, "Your God is King!"

Proverbs 4:26-27

"Survey the path for your feet, and all your ways will be sure. Turn neither to right nor to left, keep your foot far from evil."

While it is difficult for the believer to suffer injustice while watching the unjust prosper, balance has to come into perspective at some point. For the believer, even when things on this earth don't seem fair one thing remains clear, God is just. Even when evil seems to be winning the believer isn't bamboozled. They know they are still playing for the winning team because God works for the good of all those who love Him (Romans 8:28).

Isaiah 54:17

"*Every weapon*
fashioned against you
shall fail;
every tongue
that brings you to trial you
shall prove false.
This is the lot of the servants of the Lord,
their vindication *from me*
—*oracle of the Lord.*"

Notes

Works Cited

Chapter 1

Goodwin, Hannah. "Hill song LIVE sings for Christ Alone, the Cornerstone." CBN. com, 1 Jan. 2014. Web. 31 July 2014.

Perkins, Spencer, and Chris Rice. More than equals: racial healing for the sake of the gospel. 2000 ed. Downers Grove, Ill. InterVarsity Press, 1993. Print

Swanson, David. "Does Theological Cluelessness = Church Segregation?" ChurchLeaders.com. ChurchLeaders.com. Web. 22 Aug. 2014.

Chapter 2

Boardman, MD, Samantha. "Enclothed Cognition: How Clothes Can Make Us Feel Better, Smarter, and Empowered." EverydayHealth.com. Everyday Health, 1 Oct. 2012. Web. 19 July 2014. <http://www.everydayhealth.com/emotional-health/enclothed-cognition-how-clothes-can-make-us-feel-better-smarter-and-empowered.aspx>.

Chapter 3

Barnett, Brent. "Biblical Womanhood: How the Bible Defines Femininity." Revelant Bible Teaching, n.d. Web. 19 July 2014. <http://www.relevantbibleteaching.com/site/cpage.asp?cpage_id=140011648&sec_id=140001239>.

Davis, D'Ann. "A Real Woman? Defining Biblical Femininity." Living Hope Ministries, 27 July 2011. Web. 19 July 2014. <http://livehope.org/resource/a-real-woman-defining-biblical-femininity/>.

Chapter 4

http://www.forbes.com/sites/quora/2013/01/16what-is-the-difference-between-made-to-measure-and-bespoke/

Chapter 5

The Anxiety Epidemic Is Sweeping The US , Maura Kelley, The Atlantic 2012

Chapter 6

Swanson, David. "Does Theological Cluelessness = Church Segregation?" ChurchLeaders.com. ChurchLeaders.com. Web. 22 Aug. 2014.

Chapter 7

www.communityhealth.ku.edu

http://www.charismamag.com/site-archives/1570-spirit-led-woman/bible-study/9695-equally-redeemed-from-the-fall

"Terry M. Crist Wrote in a 2002 Issue of Charisma Magazine in an Article "Equally

Redeemed from the Fall": (http://www.charismamag.com/site-archives/1570-spirit-led-woman/bible-study/9695-equally-redeemed-from-the-fall)." N.p., n.d. Web.

Barnett, Brent. "Biblical Womanhood: How the Bible Defines Femininity." Relevant Bible Teaching, n.d. Web. 19 July 2014. <http://www.relevantbibleteaching.com/site/cpage.asp?cpage_id=140011648&sec_id=140001239>.

Life, Hope & Truth Magazine, John Foster (http://lifehopeandtruth.com/change/faith/women-of-faith/sarah/)

Newsome, Jean. By James Brown. *It's a Man's Man's Man's World.* King, 1966. Vinyl recording.

Chapter 8

Swanson, David. "Does Theological Cluelessness = Church Segregation?" ChurchLeaders.com. ChurchLeaders.com. Web. 22 Aug. 2014.

Chapter 9

Evans, Tony. "The Importance of your Destiny." Destiny. Eugene, Oregon: Harvest House, 2013. Print.

"The Helmet of Salvation, Part 1." David, Jeremiah. Turning Point. Dr. David Jeremiah.

23 June 2014. Radio. Spurgeon, Charles. "The Wedding Garment." Metropolitan Tabernacle Pulpit. Metropolitan Tabernacle. London, England. 19 February 1871. Speech.

Chapter 10

http://lifehopeandtruth.com/change/faith/women-of-faith/sarah

Williams, S.S., Professional Organizer, Structure with Sarah (2011). Jacksonville, FL, www.structurewithsarah.com

Chapter 11

"The Helmet of Salvation, Part 1." David, Jeremiah. Turning Point. Dr. David Jeremiah.

Chapter 12

Peter Travers, "Dark Knight," in Rolling Stone (July 18, 2008).

Chapter 13

http://wwwmigrate.usccb.org/

Small/Large Group Bible Study Guidelines

These guidelines are provisions to plan for either a large or small group of women in a church or similar setting to complete this study together. The suggestions given are the actual tools "that worked" used during a two-year pilot of the study. Deciding on specific goals that you would like to see in women's ministry program will bond the women in your small and large group setting and unify each of you to a common cause. Determining these goals will also give the women a unified sense of purpose.

For a large group of women (10 & up): Form groups of 4-8 women per group and assign a group leader. Group leaders should be a member in good standing at their local church who is adept at facilitating. Assigning a co-leader to come alongside the group leader helps to disciple new leadership and share the burden of responsibility, especially if the group is large.

For a small group of women (4-8), the study is effectively done as one body instead of the group breaking off. Although not a necessity, food does create a warm relational environment. If the study takes place during a two-hour Bible study format, it's always a great idea to come up with a consistent method to provide refreshments. In our case we met from 9:30-11:30am where our numbers were anywhere from 25-40 members. We took turns as small groups using a sign-up sheet to provide breakfast for the entire group. If the study takes place in an hour-long format then perhaps light refreshments can be shared amongst the group in the same manner.

As a group, what you'll be working on is reviewing the chapter reading that each group member should have already completed throughout that previous week. The only exception is the first meeting, which has a reflection piece the group can work on together, found at the end of Chapter 1, titled, "God was in our Midst, or was He?" Another option is to be sure participants receive their books prior to the actual start date of the study so they can read chapter 1.

The following are attainable goals for a large group (women broken off into individual small groups) and or one small group. The women in our small group will:

- Commit to learning each other's names.
- Commit to praying for each other on a weekly basis.
- Commit to attending our study regularly.
- Dedicate time during the week to study our Bibles.
- Dedicate time during the week to complete our homework.
- Strive to volunteer for one or more service projects together.
- Actively look for opportunities to invite women to our study and ministry activities.
- Develop a heart for missions outreach within the local and or global community.
- Develop an environment where trust is groomed and esteemed.
- Create a friendly and hospitable environment for other women.
- Create an atmosphere that is engaging, fun, and relational.

Sign Below:

_____

_____

_____

_____

_____

_____

_____

_____

_____

1. We will follow the general schedule with a few exceptions. Some of you may have invited friends to the study who will feel more comfortable if they are placed on your table. That is fine. However, we will randomly assign attendees to groups.

2. There will be a few icebreaker activities to help people get to know each other and or to break the ice.

3. Icebreaker #1- There will be samples of several sweets for people to take. They will be asked to write a poem about their favorite piece of candy or their least favorite. We will them create four groups of the people who liked sweets 1-4 best.

4. Icebreaker #2- During this time each person will share one highlight of their year so far and one personal goal they have for the remainder of the year.

5. Icebreaker #3- Then we'll create two groups the group who wrote the "I like" poems and the "I don't like" poems. Each group will then vote on a winner.

6. The winning poems will be read aloud. Winners get prizes.

7. After the icebreaker activities, the women will be dismissed to their small groups. The small group activity will revolve around a reflection piece written by the author of "God's Little Black Dress For Women." Begin, by reading the article with the women. Then use the discussion guide to lead the discussion. Be sure to allow time after for questions and prayer.

Leader Notes

_____

_____

_____

_____

_____

_____

_____

_____

_____

_____

_____

_____

_____

_____

_____

_____

_____

_____

_____

_____

_____

_____

Sample Agenda

1. Opening Prayer:

• Before each session opens, be sure to assign one person to pray for the entire group. If including food of any kind into your study this would be a good time to pray over the food as well.

2. Devotion/Worship:

• Prior to the study beginning, have women sign up to share a devotion based on the key scriptures presented in each chapter. It's vital to put a time limit on the devotion as well as to have a mature woman in leadership review devotions before shared with an entire group. Devotions are personal reflections based on either an event or truth experienced in an attendee's life that relates back to the Word of God. It does not have to be a divulging of extremely personal information.

• An optional addition to the program is the element of worship. If this option is doable, it does add more dynamic to the meeting time. This can be done while at a table setting. If you have the option to set a few chairs up in an area near to your tables in rows appropriate for corporate worship, this is ideal. Worship songs that include the words and music are readily available and free by downloading from an appropriate internet site. Even singing one or two songs together can change the atmosphere to one that is sacred, focused and unified. During this time, don't forget the power of personal touch. Before we'd dismiss to our small groups we'd give each other welcome hugs. Then we'd do what we referred to as seated or standing, "train massages." For about 3-5 minutes, we'd take the time to turn in our seats or get up and give the person in front of us a back rub, while getting one! Then we'd turn around and reverse our line. This is a great way to distress and add the fun factor!

3. Review key scripture:
• Each chapter focuses in key scripture in the participant guides. Be sure to review the scripture. Posting it in an area everyone can see is a good reminder to pay attention to this important element. Encourage women to commit the memory verse to memory.

4. Checking in:

• Daily News: briefly have participants in their small groups share regarding their personal lives.
• Review the homework for session.
• Share prayer concerns/praise reports

5. Highlight the following points:

• Using the teaching highlights at the end of each chapter, review the teaching points from the past chapter.

6. Group discussion questions:

• Using the two, group discussion questions found in the leader's guide, encourage each woman to share.

7. Prayer board exchange:

• Using some type of simple display board that is either portable or stationary, have women post prayer requests on a board. Then each woman takes a prayer off to pray for someone else during the week.

8. Closing prayer:

• Close out in prayer within small group (if your study is made of 10 or more women meeting in individual groups).